Lewis Latimer,
THE FIRST HIDDEN FIGURE

Also by Steve Mitnick

Lines Down
How We Pay, Use, Value Grid Electricity Amid the Storm

Lewis Latimer, The First Hidden Figure

By Steve Mitnick

Public Utilities Fortnightly
Lines Up, Inc.
Arlington, Virginia

Library of Congress Control Number: 2020947176

Author: Steve Mitnick
Editor: Lori Burkhart
Assistant Editor: Angela Hawkinson
Production: Mike Eacott
Cover Design: Paul Kjellander
Illustrations: Dennis Auth
Dust jacket back cover texture: © Can Stock Photo / ArtesiaWells

For information, contact:

Lines Up, Inc.
3033 Wilson Blvd
Suite 700
Arlington, VA 22201

First Printing, November 2020

ISBN 978-1-7360142-1-9

Printed in the United States of America.

To my boyhood heroes
Satchel Paige,
Jackie Robinson,
Elston Howard
and Al Downing

Table of Contents

List of Illustrations and Patent Excerpts

Lewis Latimer early in his career

USS Massasoit, the steam side-wheel gunboat Lewis Latimer served on during the Civil War

Lewis Latimer in the middle of his career

Lewis Latimer's 1881 electric lamp patent, with Joseph V. Nichols

Lewis Latimer's 1882 process of manufacturing carbons patent

Edison Electric Light Co. headquarters at 65 Fifth Avenue in Manhattan, where Lewis Latimer started working in Edison's Engineering Department in 1884

Edison General Electric Co.'s new headquarters at 42 Broad Street in Manhattan, where Lewis Latimer worked in the Law Department starting in 1890

Edison's Law Department including Lewis Latimer

Lewis Latimer as an elder statesman of electricity's development

Edison Pioneers meet for the first time, including Lewis Latimer

Edison Pioneers meet with Thomas Edison, including Lewis Latimer

The illustrations within this book were created by Public Utilities Fortnightly artist Dennis Auth.

List of Tables

Lewis Latimer's Patents

Cited U.S. Supreme Court Decisions

A Word of Inspiration
by David Owens

The author of this book is very pleased to offer to you, the reader, a word of inspiration by David K. Owens. Known throughout our community of utilities and utility regulation, he is the retired executive vice president of the Edison Electric Institute, and is presently a board member at Xcel Energy and co-chair of the transformation advisory council at the Puerto Rico Electric Power Authority. Public Utilities Fortnightly celebrated his illustrious career with our first Owen Young Award, PUF's highest honor, in 2018.

And now, a word of inspiration by David:

This superb writing heightened my awareness about the courage and greatness of Lewis Latimer. My career pales to his. While there are significant differences in our intellect and accomplishments, we have a lot in common. We have both been devoted husbands; we have strong faith; we want to make a positive difference in people's lives; and we want to leave a legacy of accomplishments. I also realize that the myriad challenges Lewis Latimer faced are not dissimilar to those faced by many men of color.

There are other similarities we share. Lewis Latimer was the man behind the scenes; he provided the limelight so others could shine. He was guided by humility, not arrogance, as many of his white contemporaries. The loudest voice in the room is not always the sharpest and most insightful. Latimer knew the answers, but his quiet demeanor did not draw attention to his brilliance and vision. Like him, many of us remain in the shadows sometimes never being appropriately recognized for our contributions by those who feel superior or threatened by a person of color. How unfortunate! That is not an excuse for not striving for excellence.

Lewis Latimer was the son of a freed slave. Changes in the political landscape forced his father into hiding to avoid being re-enslaved. Lewis witnessed his father's tenacity and strong commitment to make a better life for his family as a freedman. That struggle became embedded in Latimer's being. We all have similar stories.

My drive generates from three strong black women — my grandmother who migrated from North Carolina in the late thirties; her father was an indentured servant. While she only had a first grade education, she was the wisest most giving person I have ever met. I get my tenacity from her. My mother won a scholarship to A&T College. She had to drop out to work because the family was very poor. My mother was brilliant with numbers and in finance. The third strong woman who helped shape my life is my late beloved wife. She was a tremendous mother to my three children and my biggest cheerleader. She gave me inspiration, support, and true love. Along with my strong faith, I am forever indebted to them.

Like many black families, my father who served in the Navy, had great difficulty getting a fair paying job to sustain his family. He died when I was nine years old. It is important for me to tell you this so you will never stop believing that you can do anything you put your mind to. Never stop believing you can achieve! Latimer left school after the fifth grade. He taught himself drafting, and electrical engineering, and became fluent in French, German, Latin, and Greek.

We are in the midst of a significant movement that Black Lives Matter stimulated by the brutal death of George Floyd captured on video for all the world to see. This movement helps me reflect on the struggle for Civil Rights during my activism in the sixties and seventies. I witnessed the anger, frustration and rioting following the assassination of Dr. Martin Luther King and the dashed hopes for equality and justice. Voting rights, equal housing and other landmark legislation have passed only to be weakened by systemic racism. Black Lives Matter is a movement. Speak up and speak out!

During my career I have come to understand the importance to be surrounded by positive people who can impart wisdom, support, and guidance in your life. Lewis Latimer became well acquainted with The Who's Who of people of color during his time. They inspired him and grounded and enhanced his pride as a man of color. These giants helped contribute to his strength, perseverance, and commitment to excellence. They also stressed the importance of reaching back to help others. It is noteworthy that Latimer was the only black man in the elite circle of the Edison Pioneers.

I have benefitted from association with established and evolving black leaders in science, engineering, business, and technology in the American Association of Blacks in Energy (AABE). AABE has enhanced my network, knowledge, and self-esteem. I have been an active member for over forty years. I am fortunate to have met many of its founders — men of great pride and stature. As the first African American to hold an officer position at the Edison Electric Institute, AABE has been instrumental in my success. Prior to my retirement, I served as Chair of the Legislative Issues and Public Policy Committee and helped spearhead AABE's significant input into major energy legislation such as the Energy Policy Acts of 1992 and 2005 and various clean energy legislation.

I have the high honor of being the twice recipient of the James E. Stewart Award, the highest distinction for an American Association of Blacks in Energy member. Participation in AABE taught me to be unfailingly generous with my time and knowledge to mentor young men and women in their energy careers. It is important to give back!

It also is important to become active in the movement for real change to end systemic racism in America.

Now is the time!!

Sponsoring this Book and the PUF Latimer Scholarship Fund

Rather than for sale, this book is being distributed freely throughout the Public Utilities Fortnightly community due to the generous support of some highly-respected organizations of our community. These utilities and firms – CPS Energy, Dentons, Energy Impact Partners, FirstEnergy, Guidehouse, Xcel Energy – believe as does this author that Lewis Latimer's life informs and inspires contemporary leaders of the electric industry. That Black Lives Matter. That our industry and society progresses most when peoples of all colors and backgrounds are treated respectfully, equally and justly, are allowed to fulfill their potential, and are enabled to fully apply their energies and talents. Please see the moving statements by the sponsoring organizations on the following pages.

The sponsoring organizations are additionally dedicating a substantial portion of their support to jump-start the PUF Latimer Scholarship Fund, a new source of financial support for African American students, to be administered by American Association of Blacks in Energy. AABE, in partnership with Public Utilities Fortnightly, will seek and provide support to students who personify Lewis Latimer's dedication to developing the necessary skills to further advance technology in the service of the public interest.

Founded in 1977, AABE serves as a resource for policy discussions of the energy and environmental impacts on African Americans and other minorities, ensures involvement of African Americans in energy policymaking, encourages the public and private sectors to be responsive to the energy problems, goals and aspirations of African Americans, and encourages African American students to pursue careers in energy. For more information, see AABE's website, at aabe.org.

Moving Statements by the Sponsoring Organizations

The life, ingenious mind, and resiliency of Lewis Latimer should make us *all* proud. Mr. Latimer's journey is an amazing story of someone who refused to let his spirit be doused. Every day, he chose to never let the anger of oppression shut him down, or shut him off. He was THE original lemonade maker, taking the mountains of lemons given to him in life and turning them into sweet success. What he did is incredibly inspirational – to choose to be positive and move forward no matter how poorly he was treated the day before.

Sadly, during his lifetime, no one gave him the formal and clear recognition he deserved. That makes this book an incredible opportunity for people to get acquainted with Lewis Latimer and the legacy he created, which today benefits everyone. It grounds me to think often of trailblazers who came before me, and if not specifically for Mr. Latimer, I may not be in the position I am today. He is a previously unsung, but now recognized, hero whose story will inspire me in the days and years to come. As the only African American female CEO of a large utility in the nation, or for that matter the globe, I fully embrace my refreshed responsibility to pay it forward. It is my privilege to continue to make way for those who will follow in my footsteps, as Mr. Latimer has done for me.

It is always important to remember the past and, in this case, seek more understanding of the history we did not know before. In addition to understanding the painful parts of our history, we must celebrate our predecessors' perseverance, indelible spirits, creativity, and intellect.

CPS Energy, representing 3,100 dedicated energy professionals, is proud to support this new publication, *Lewis Latimer, the First Hidden Figure*, by Steve Mitnick, as well as Public Utilities Fortnightly's (PUF) Latimer Scholarship Fund. We thank Steve and PUF, for passionately telling Mr. Latimer's wonderful story and for always advocating for the just evolution of our utility industry and the many talented people who work in it every day.

> – Paula Gold-Williams, Chief Executive Officer, CPS Energy

Someone once wrote that history is littered with promises unfulfilled. This certainly is true with regard to the promise of our Declaration of Independence "...that all Men are created equal, that they are endowed by their Creator with certain unalienable Rights, that among these are Life, Liberty, and the Pursuit of Happiness."

The ugly history of slavery and injustice, systemic racism and social inequity in our Country is finally receiving the multiracial examination that is essential if we are to move forward as a more unified nation. Now it is time to get purposeful.

The remarkable life, inventions and achievements of Lewis Howard Latimer have largely been invisible, eclipsed by his white "teammates" Thomas Edison and Alexander Graham Bell. It is stunning how much Lewis Latimer accomplished professionally and humanistically on such an appallingly uneven playing field.

The Dentons Law Firm is honored to co-sponsor this extraordinary biography written by my dear friend Steve Mitnick and I am so impressed and grateful for his selfless effort. As Steve writes: "...our industry and society progresses when peoples of all color and backgrounds are treated respectfully, equally, and justly, are allowed to fulfill their potential and are enabled to fully apply their energy and talents." We also are deeply honored to contribute to the PUF Latimer Scholarship Fund creating a new source of revenue for African American students.

It is also moving to read the Foreword by our friend and energy industry hero David Owen. We echo his call to action: "It is important to become active in the movement for real change to end systemic racism in America. Now is the Time!!"

Truly so David. We are all in this together.

> – Clinton A. Vince, Chair, Dentons' US Energy Practice,
> and Co-Chair, Dentons' Global Energy Sector

Energy Impact Partners (EIP) is proud to be a founding co-sponsor of the Lewis Latimer biography by Steve Mitnick and the PUF Latimer Scholarship Fund.

Innovation should be color blind, but as Steve Mitnick's book points out oftentimes black entrepreneurs, like Lewis Latimer, do not have the resources (money, mentorship and network) to execute, perfect or protect their original ideas. Seven patents are directly attributable to Latimer.

Another three have him listed as a co-party witness. An amazing feat for a black man who was self-taught with no resources working just after the Civil War. But as Mitnick's book suggests, Latimer could have very many more patents to his name. Indeed, Latimer may have had the winning hand in the patent fight with Thomas Edison to electrify the country if he had the lawyers to continue the battle. Imagine where this country would be today if Latimer and not Edison had won that patent battle?

EIP's support for the launch of the Latimer book and scholarship fund is one small step to bring more assistance to black and underrepresented minorities in the venture capital sector. We have a lot more to do and believe our unique model of innovation portends greater opportunity for blacks and under-represented minorities.

– Kevin C. Fitzgerald, Chief Utility Officer, Energy Impact Partners

FirstEnergy is proud to support the publication and distribution of this book commemorating Lewis Latimer, who made enormous contributions to the early electric industry and helped to advance American society through curiosity, innovation and invention.

Lewis Latimer succeeded in making advancements as an inventor and innovator despite the most unjust circumstances, only to then be erased from public memory. His life and work have remained obscured from view for far too long, and we're grateful to Steve Mitnick for illuminating his untold story and highlighting his achievements in science and engineering. This book educates us about the past and corrects Latimer's absence from the historical record, but it also motivates us to keep pushing for racial equity, justice and diversity.

How many Lewis Latimers are we missing because we excluded them from opportunities or denied them recognition? Racial discrimination, exclusion and bias are very real problems in our country and have been for decades. It's time for all of us, especially leaders, to correct those problems. We believe that if we focus on our respective spheres of influence, commit to building racial diversity, equity and inclusion, and hold ourselves accountable to making progress, then we can foster real, positive change.

At FirstEnergy, we're determined to create a more diverse and inclusive company and to ensure opportunities for advancement and development at all levels of our organization – from employees who are just starting their careers to those on our leadership team. That's why we're proud to support the PUF Latimer Scholarship Fund, a new source of financial support for Black students interested in pursuing careers in the energy industry. It is our hope that Lewis Latimer's story and this scholarship fund will help ensure that any motivated students can imagine a future for themselves as creators, inventors and innovators and reach their full potential in our industry.

– FirstEnergy Corporation

Guidehouse is honored to support this amazing book by our dear friend, Steve Mitnick, as he tells the remarkable and unforgettable – yet not always remembered – story of Lewis Howard Latimer.

We should all know and learn about Latimer's unsung contributions to the advancement of the electric industry, as they are especially worthy of celebrating during this time of global awakening around the true costs of racial injustice. Lisa Cook, a renowned black economist, published her findings around the significant impacts of racism on innovation, quantifying the losses in billions of dollars and thousands of "lost" inventions that racial violence and oppression cost our nation and humankind.

While our recognition of Latimer is not timely, nor nearly enough, to celebrate his monumental contributions, it's a positive step toward creating a new environment in which innovation is a little less bound by misguided concepts of who has the capacity to make great and innovative contributions to society.

Innovation has played a major role in solving a wide range of problems. Today, it plays a crucial role as we are faced with problems that feel bigger than ever before, or even existential, like reversing climate change. Innovation has and will further impact governments, businesses, and people all over the world. Latimer was one of the founding fathers of innovation, and we are glad that Steve decided to tell his story.

– Jan Vrins, Global Energy, Sustainability and Infrastructure Segment Leader, Guidehouse

Lewis Latimer already had been awarded the first of seven patents when he was only 25 years old. An impressive feat for anyone, but particularly for the son of slaves who had fled Virginia and moved north six years before his birth in 1848.

Latimer, an engineer and inventor, went on to become a true pioneer in the electricity industry. Xcel Energy is now excited to support the publication of this book, which honors this man who made enormous contributions to our industry. Those include achieving an important patent to improve early versions of the light bulb, authoring the first-ever book on electric lighting, and supervising the installation of public electric lights in New York, Philadelphia, Montreal and London.

Beyond his impressive body of work, Latimer also had a prescient view of the future. "There must be vistas flying out beyond, that promise more than present conditions yield," he once said. Latimer spent his life working toward those vistas, helping Black America slowly emerge from the days of slavery and move toward freedom – despite hardships faced every step of the way.

Indeed, our country has a long history of disservice to the Black community. Part of our reconciliation process now is the need to understand and appreciate the contributions of Black Americans to our society – regardless of whether those contributions are current or centuries old. I'm thankful that Steve Mitnick researched and wrote the story of Lewis Latimer. It is one of many stories that need to be told and appreciated not just within the electricity industry, but throughout society.

As chairman of the Edison Electric Institute, an important part of my platform is to improve diversity and inclusion throughout the industry. We will redouble diversity and inclusion initiatives to hire, retain and advocate for Black employees and other people of color – and celebrate their important contributions to our success.

– Ben Fowke, Chief Executive Officer, Xcel Energy, and Chairman,
Edison Electric Institute

Acknowledgements

I could not have undertaken the extensive research and writing – with the greatest care for the noble soul that is the subject of this book, Lewis Latimer – without the extraordinary support of my staff at Lines Up, Inc. and Public Utilities Fortnightly, Lori Burkhart, Mike Eacott, Angela Hawkinson, Kevaghn Hinkley, Joe Paparello and Alexandra Revel. They took up the slack as I spent uncountable hours working on this book which inevitably pulled me away, somewhat, from working with them on our small company's core tasks.

It is also important to thank the many PUF member organizations who continue to financially support Public Utilities Fortnightly so faithfully through their annual membership fees. They provide the seed from which we are able to grow works such as this book.

Next, I wish to express my gratitude to the director and general editor of the Thomas A. Edison Papers at Rutgers University, Paul B. Israel, and the staff of the Association of Edison Illuminating Companies. They graciously provided me a deeper understanding of Edison's operations during the period when Lewis Latimer was at a competing firm, when Latimer was at Edison's firm, and when Latimer worked at successor firms.

And, finally, I thank my many friends in the leadership of utilities, utility associations, and utility regulatory commissions who are African American. When the events of this spring transpired, that once again called into question our society's justice for all, I thought of these friends, which is what inspired me to write this book.

Steve Mitnick

Note to Readers

Some of the quotes in this book were and are offensive, and some of the author's text describe events in American history that none of us can be proud of. These quotes and text are included in the book in order to offer the reader a deeper understanding of the challenges and the racism that Lewis Latimer and all African Americans for that matter faced during Latimer's lifetime in the second half of the nineteenth century and first quarter of the twentieth century.

Lewis Latimer's Patents

Lewis Latimer received seven patents. Three of these were received with a co-inventor.

Additionally, he witnessed two of Hiram Maxim's patents, and was assigned a half interest in a patent received by another inventor. It's probable Latimer had a significant role in all three of these patents as well.

The ten patents are:

Water-Closets for Railroad-Cars. Patent number 147,363. Applied January 14, 1874 and issued to Latimer on February 10 of that year. Co-inventor with Latimer: Charles W. Brown.

Electric Lamp. Patent number 247,097. Applied April 18, 1881 and issued September 13 of that year. Co-inventor with Latimer: Joseph V. Nichols.

Process of Manufacturing Carbons. Patent number 252,386. Applied February 19, 1881 and issued to Latimer on January 17 of the next year. Assigned to Hiram Maxim's company, United States Electric Lighting Co.

Globe Supporter for Electric Lamps. Patent number 255,212. Applied September 7, 1881 and issued March 21 of the next year. Co-inventor with Latimer: John Tregoning. Also assigned to Maxim's company, U.S. Electric Lighting Co.

Apparatus for Cooling and Disinfecting. Patent number 334,078. Applied September 3, 1885 and issued to Latimer on January 12 of the next year. Witnessed by Latimer's wife Mary.

Locking Rack for Hats, Coats, Umbrellas, &c. Patent number 557,076. Applied August 25, 1895 and issued to Latimer on March 24 of the next year.

Book Supporter. Patent number 781,890. Applied June 3, 1904 and issued to Latimer on February 7 of the next year.

Process of Manufacturing Carbon Conductors. Patent number 230,309. Applied March 22, 1880 and issued to Maxim on July 20 of that year. Witnessed by Latimer.

Electric Lamp. Patent number 237,198. Applied March 9, 1880 and issued to Maxim on February 1 of the next year. Witnessed by Latimer.

Lamp-Fixture. Patent number 968,787. Applied August 23, 1909 and issued to William S. Norton on August 30 of the next year. Witnessed by Latimer.

Cited U.S. Supreme Court Decisions

This book refers to seven important decisions by the U.S. Supreme Court. What follows is a brief summary of their impact on the racial inequities that Lewis Latimer among millions encountered:

Dred Scott versus Sandford. Decided March 6, 1857. Causing George Latimer to hide from potential slave catchers, at a time when his youngest son Lewis Latimer was eight-and-a-half years old.

From "Arguing Until Doomsday: Stephen Douglas, Jefferson Davis, and the Struggle for American Democracy" by Michael E. Woods:

"[President] Buchanan counted on the Supreme Court to derail antislavery activism … In his inaugural address [in 1857], Buchanan alluded to a decision that would end the Kansas controversy and 'speedily and finally' settle the question of timing — when could territorial voters decide on slavery? … Buchanan promised to abide by the decision, whatever it said; in fact, he already knew the outcome thanks to covert communications with several justices.

Shortly thereafter, when the Court ruled 7-2 against [Dred] Scott's bid for freedom, Chief Justice Roger B. Taney sought to chisel proslavery dogma into American jurisprudence … Taney insisted that African Americans could not be citizens, for they had always 'been regarded as beings of an inferior order … and so inferior that they had no rights which the white man was bound to respect.'"

Nixon versus Condon. Decided May 2, 1932. Three-and-a-half years after Lewis Latimer passed away.

Texas' Democratic Party argued that it was "merely a voluntary association" that had the power to prohibit blacks from voting in its elections. Speaking for the 5-4 majority of the Court, Justice Benjamin N. Cardozo:

State officials may not "discharge their official functions in such a way as to discriminate invidiously between white citizens and black."

Nixon versus Herndon. Decided March 7, 1927. Nine months before Lewis Latimer passed away.

Speaking for the unanimous Court, Justice Oliver Wendell Holmes:

"The {Fourteenth Amendment} … was passed, as we know, with a special intent to protect the blacks from discrimination against them … The statute of Texas … assumes to forbid negroes to take part in a primary election the importance of which we have indicated, discriminating against them by the distinction of color alone … it is too clear for extended argument that color cannot be made the basis of a statutory classification affecting the right [to vote] set up in this case."

Plessy versus Ferguson. Decided May 18, 1896. When Lewis Latimer, at age forty-eight, was the top expert at the Board of Patent Control set up by the companies of Thomas Edison and George Westinghouse.

From "Separate: The Story of Plessy v. Ferguson, and America's Journey from Slavery to Segregation" by Steve Luxenberg:

"The ruling in Plessy drew little attention at the time, but its baneful effects lasted longer than any other civil rights decision in American history. It gave legal cover to an increasingly pernicious series of discriminatory laws in the first half of the twentieth century. Under the banner of keeping the races apart, much of white America stood silent as black Americans suffered beatings, assaults, and murders. Lynching, already a weapon of vengeance and vigilante justice in the years before the Plessy decision, became a signature tool for white bent on domination and repression."

Prigg versus Pennsylvania. Decided March 1, 1842. Seven months before George Latimer (and his wife Rebecca) escaped slavery in Virginia, arriving in Boston four days later, only to be imprisoned after four more days on the charge of "stealing himself."

From "The War Before the War: Fugitive Slaves and the Struggle for America's Soul from the Revolution to the Civil War" by Andrew Delbanco:

"Writing for the high court on March 1, 1842, Justice Joseph Story found the 1926 Pennsylvania personal liberty law unconstitutional… Story went on to declare that 'any state law or state regulation, which interrupt, limits, delays, or postpones the right of the owner to the immediate possession of the slave, and the immediate command of his service and labour' was invalid.

It was a bombshell. The Court had effectively struck down all legislative efforts by northern states to impede the fugitive slave clause of the Constitution. All protections for accused runaways had been swept away, including provisions for due process set out in the personal liberty laws."

Smith versus Allwright. Decided April 3, 1944. Fifteen-and-a-half years after Lewis Latimer passed away.

Speaking for the 8-1 majority of the Court, Justice Stanley F. Reed ruled that state primary elections must be open to voters of all races. It was what Thurgood Marshall considered his most important case, before becoming the first African American member of the high court.

United States versus Cruikshank. Decided May 27, 1876. A little more than three months after Lewis Latimer helped Alexander Graham Bell submit his application to the federal government for the telephone patent.

From "Reconstruction: America's Unfinished Revolution, 1863-1877" by Eric Foner:

"The first pivotal decision, in the Slaughterhouse Cases, was announced in 1873 … The Fourteenth Amendment, [Justice Samuel F.] Miller [speaking for the five-man majority] declared, had not fundamentally altered traditional federalism; most of the rights of citizens remained under state control, and with these the Amendment had 'nothing to do.'…

Even more devastating was the 1876 decision in U.S. v. Cruikshank … In the name of federalism, the decision rendered national prosecution of crimes committed against blacks virtually impossible, and gave the green light to acts of terror where local officials either could not or would not enforce the law."

Foreword

In Latimer's later years, he knew and often hosted at his Queen Anne-style frame house in the Flushing neighborhood of Queens, New York, purchased in 1903, the great black intellectuals of the early twentieth century. Including civil rights leaders Booker T. Washington and W.E.B. Du Bois, eight years and twenty years younger than Latimer respectively. Including the scientist George Washington Carver, sixteen years younger than Latimer. The actor and musician Paul Robeson was a guest too at the Latimer home, though fifty years younger than the man who had collaborated in the last century with Bell, Maxim and Edison.

Lewis Latimer had achieved at the highest levels of the white-dominated world of invention, engineering and business. Indeed, he was virtually the sole black professional in that world. And yet, while he was recognized for his achievements and intellect, oftentimes reluctantly, he was as well respected by the leading black intellectuals of that time.

Not too bad for a self-taught industrial draftsman, patent expert, electrical engineer, inventor, and senior manager of white men, mainly, in the U.S., Canada and England. Plus, a self-taught poet, musician (flute player), painter and master of multiple languages.

Latimer had become one of the wealthier African Americans in the early twentieth century. Although his means were modest as compared with most of the white men who worked with him and likely many that he supervised.

He integrated in white society even as he worked for civil rights. Latimer's home was in a predominantly white neighborhood. He was active in Flushing's Unitarian church attended by whites for the most part. He was an enthusiastic patriot and an adjutant in the Grand Army of the Republic, the Civil War veterans organization of mostly white men. He was famously the only black member of the Edison Pioneers, an exclusive club of Thomas Edison confidants. So easily did Latimer move between worlds, crossing borders that were closed to most.

Introduction

It is nearly impossible to adequately summarize this man's life. Lewis Howard Latimer was seemingly in the middle of everything in the second half of the nineteenth century and the first quarter of the twentieth century. And, he was seemingly in the middle of everything with everyone of prominence during this formative period in the nation's history.

Latimer played a remarkable and almost inexplicable role in the period. We are reminded of the hero of the 1986 book, and the 1994 film, Forrest Gump. But that character, played masterfully by actor Tom Hanks, was fictional. Latimer was real.

As an impoverished teenager, with only a fifth grade education, Latimer enlisted to become a gunboat seaman in the Civil War. In his late twenties, after teaching himself industrial drawing, patent law and electrical engineering, Latimer helped Alexander Graham Bell get the credit for the telephone invention, barely beating out Bell's competitors, Elisha Gray and Thomas Edison among them.

In his early thirties, Latimer helped Hiram Maxim invent electric lighting. Though, this time, Latimer's man lost the race. As any schoolchild knows, Thomas Edison got the credit instead. Maxim then gave up working on the development of the electric industry, to invent the machine gun of all things. This switch sidelined Latimer, temporarily, despite having achieved so much.

How mankind communicated had been transformed, by Bell in February of 1876. When and where that happened, Latimer was right there. And, how mankind saw in the darkness of the night, and indoors in the daytime, had been transformed too, by Edison in December of 1879, less than four years later. When and where that happened, Latimer was right there once again, kind of. For Edison barely beat out Maxim, who had hired Latimer on the spot to seize back the momentum a few months later.

Did we forget to mention Latimer's several patented inventions of his own? And, did we neglect to say that he taught himself French to more effectively direct the introduction of electric lighting to Montreal, and later added German to his repertoire to better prosecute Edison's patent rights internationally?

In Latimer's late thirties, with Maxim off in London inventing implements of war, Edison now wanted Latimer's help. So, Edison went ahead and hired Latimer. In 1884, Latimer started working at 65 Fifth Avenue in Manhattan, the four-story brownstone that had become Edison's headquarters three years earlier. 65 Fifth Avenue was the first building to be lit exclusively by electricity. This historic structure was later demolished, and then was the site for a department store that featured women's hats, and now is the site for a New School college building.

Before hiring Latimer, Edison waited until the conclusion of a lawsuit that he had brought against Latimer. That's right. Three years earlier, Edison alleged a Latimer patent application on electric lighting infringed on one of his own. At issue was the connection of a light bulb's filament to the electrical wire. Edison's relentless legal team outgunned Latimer's legal representation of course, if indeed Latimer had any.

By his early forties, Latimer had risen to become a star of Edison's team that strove to monopolize the rapidly-growing global electricity industry. And, in his fifties, Latimer led the joint efforts of the Edison companies and those of George Westinghouse, now the main rival, to assert their primacy in and monopoly over the patents of all things electric.

And then, in his later years, as an elder statesman of sorts, Latimer moved somewhat seamlessly between the giants of American business and invention and the giants of African American culture and civil rights. Oh! There's something about Latimer that I have not yet noted.

Daunting and Daily Barriers

Latimer was an African American. Which makes all his accomplishments that much more remarkable considering the daunting and daily barriers that any black of the period needed to hurdle.

Indeed, how Latimer was so successful, and how he was able to contribute so much in his lifetime, battling impossible odds, is almost unfathomable. For Latimer was an African American at a very troubled time in the nation's convoluted road to racial equality. He managed nonetheless, through grit, genius and guile, to crash through glass ceiling after glass ceiling, and to sit in some of the most prestigious circles of American commerce. In those exclusive rooms were men (and yes, they were all men), who likely knew no other colleague of color aside from Latimer.

Even Latimer's childhood was extraordinary. His father's flight from slavery in 1842, and the city of Boston's ferocious fight against his father's former slave master who expected to forcefully return George Latimer to bondage in Virginia, was the first skirmish in the abolitionist movement and the march to the Civil War and Emancipation.

It apparently didn't slow down Lewis Latimer that much when the U.S. Supreme Court handed down the disastrous Dred Scott versus Sandford decision on March 6, 1857, when young Lewis was just eight and a half years old, and about four years before the southern states seceded from the union. Chief Justice Roger Brooke Taney's majority opinion forced Lewis' father George to go into hiding, in the genuine fear of recapture by slavers, leaving behind Lewis, his mother Rebecca – who had escaped slavery with his father – and his two brothers and sister. The family had no choice but to break apart. And, the studious Lewis had no choice too but to abandon his schooling to earn his keep.

Latimer wasn't slowed when the south's Reconstruction suffered a still-birth in the winter of 1876-1877, setting back the entire nation's estimation of racial equality, when Latimer was twenty-eight years old. And, he wasn't slowed when the Jim Crow laws and lynching increasingly ravaged the south amid widespread apathy elsewhere in the nation. And, he wasn't slowed when the Supreme Court handed down the Plessy versus Ferguson decision in 1896, when Latimer was forty-eight, enshrining segregation nationally.

Latimer was relentlessly striving to achieve more and contribute more, notwithstanding the biases and worse against men and women of his skin color. It is so telling that at age seventy-five, Latimer actually made a serious attempt and came fairly close to becoming the first black producer of a major movie.

How could a man do all this? Particularly at a time when white America generally knew of no more than a handful of blacks at the apex of their fields: Frederick Douglass, W.E.B. Du Bois, George Washington Carver, Harriet Tubman, Booker T. Washington, and Ida Wells. And, particularly at a time when so many whites resented the achievements of even these admirable figures.

One keeps coming back to that most basic fact about this man, Lewis Latimer. He was indeed relentlessly striving to achieve more and contribute more.

Of the Colored Race, the Only One in Our Organization

Latimer died on December 11, 1928. In his last full year, the Supreme Court had decided the landmark case of Nixon versus Herndon. On March 27, 1927, the highest court in the land ruled that the Texas legislature's so-called white primary law, passed four years earlier – in which blacks were barred from participating in the primary of the dominant party, the Democrats – violated the equal protection clause of the Fourteenth Amendment. The unanimous opinion was written by Associate Justice Oliver Wendell Holmes, Jr.

Of course, the Texas legislature then promptly passed a new law empowering the party's executive committee to limit eligibility to whites. In 1932, this action by Texans was also struck down by the Supreme Court, in Nixon versus Condon. And wouldn't you know it? Texas Democrats then banned blacks from the party, even after the two Supreme Court decisions. Eventually, the 1944 Supreme Court decision in Smith versus Allwright put an end to the white primary.

In the year of Latimer's death, that spring, Secretary of Commerce and soon to be President Herbert Hoover, took the controversial step of desegregating the Census Bureau. Southern newspapers and politicians went crazy. Senator H.D. Stephens of Mississippi wrote to Hoover:

"... your knowledge of human nature and your sense of decency and propriety must cause you to know that the breasts of many of the employees in the bureau are seething with unuttered protests against the condition that you have brought about … History can not be trifled with. Whenever there has been a step towards social equality between the races, dire results have followed, and both races have suffered."

After Hoover disavowed his action in large part and attempted to pacify Southern white voters in the presidential election that year, African American leaders finally turned for good from the Republican party. Hoover was nevertheless elected a few weeks before Latimer passed away, in a landslide carrying every state except six in the deep south, and Massachusetts and Rhode Island where Catholics clung to the first Catholic presidential candidate, Al Smith, the Democrats' standard-bearer. In Hoover's re-election run, in 1932, black voters embraced the Democratic party in unprecedented numbers, supporting that party's nominee, Franklin Delano Roosevelt.

It is most telling what the Edison Pioneers wrote in their eulogy when Latimer passed away. The Edison Pioneers was the all-white elite club of some of the most successful businessmen and inventors of the Second Industrial Revolution. That is, it was all-white with the lone exception, Latimer. The eulogy includes these poignant lines:

"He was of the colored race, the only one in our organization, and was one of those to respond to the initial call that led to the formation of the Edison Pioneers, January 24th, 1918. Broadmindedness, versatility in the accomplishment of things intellectual and cultural, a linguist, a devoted husband and father, all were characteristic of him, and his genial presence will be missed from our gatherings … We hardly mourn his inevitable going so much as we rejoice in pleasant memory at having been associated with him in a great work for all peoples under a great man [Thomas Edison]."

Chapter One

The First Hidden Figure

First, and Alone

We call it the Great Migration. As many as six million African Americans abandoned their homes in the south after several decades of terrible hardship and violence there, even after slavery's end. They uprooted and moved to the north (what we now call the northeast), to the midwest, and to the west. But, we must recall, that this historic exodus didn't begin in earnest until the nineteen-teens, around the time that the country entered World War I.

So, the Great Migration took place long after some of the most transformational inventors in history worked. Alexander Graham Bell. Hiram Maxim. Thomas Edison. Each changed the world. Each found fame and fortune. And, to do so, each of these men entrusted an African American of the north. Born free in Massachusetts, though his parents had fled bondage from Virginia, Lewis Latimer's ethnicity was quite unusual to most northerners.

In those years, prior to the Great Migration, relatively few blacks lived in Massachusetts, or in other northern states such as Connecticut and New York. The demographics of these three states in particular are important to grasp in order to understand Latimer's life. For these states are where Bell, Maxim and Edison invented the telephone and electric lighting in the eighteen-seventies and eighteen-eighties.

According to the 1880 Census, African Americans were just one and six-tenths percent of all northerners, so they constituted a very small minority. In comparison, thirty-six percent of all southerners were black. That comes to over a third of the south's populous.

In the state of Connecticut, for instance, where Latimer worked on electric lighting with Maxim, the total black population was a little over eleven thousand. The white population was nearly six hundred and eleven thousand. In other words, there was just one black citizen for every fifty-six white citizens.

To put this into perspective, in today's America, only five states – Idaho, Montana, Utah, Vermont and Wyoming – have smaller percentages of African-Americans. Three of these states – Utah, Vermont and Wyoming – have only slightly smaller percentages than Connecticut circa 1880.

The black minority where Latimer lived, worked and succeeded was indeed a very small minority. This makes Latimer's amazing story even more amazing.

Probably no more than three-quarters of the blacks living in the communities of Boston, Bridgeport and Manhattan, where Bell's, Maxim's and Edison's labs were located, were literate in those years according to the Census. So, we should not be surprised when we find that many of the white men that worked with Latimer were surprised – and sometimes delighted and sometimes resentful – by what they commonly called their colleague, a colored man.

A Time of Firsts

It was a time of firsts for blacks trying to succeed in American society. In the decade of the eighteen-seventies, when Alexander Graham Bell would come to depend upon Latimer, Richard Theodore Greener became the first African-American to graduate from Harvard College. Harvard had admitted Greener to attend the prestigious school as "an experiment."

Greener and Latimer would eventually become good friends. And, Greener went on to become the law school's dean at Howard University, then led the fundraising to erect Grant's Tomb, and later was appointed by President William McKinley to serve as the country's General Consul in Bombay, India.

At about the same time, Edward Alexander Bouchet became the first African-American to earn a doctorate in the U.S., a Yale University Ph.D. in Physics, no less. That same year, 1876, Bell was awarded the patent for the telephone's invention with Latimer at his side.

So, yes, it was a time of firsts for blacks trying to succeed in American society. But for Latimer, his career was already well underway, and he was now entering his peak period of innovation and invention.

We all know of the great Frederick Douglass, who regularly conferred with presidents, starting with Abraham Lincoln. Douglass was one of the very few black intellectuals generally known and respected by the predominantly white American public in the eighteen-seventies. He was already fifty-six years old when Latimer earned his first patent in 1874, as a twenty-six year old.

There was the serial black inventor, Granville Tailer Woods. He became fairly well known as "the Black Edison." But Woods was eight years younger than Latimer, and he didn't earn his first patent until 1884 – for a steam boiler furnace – ten years after Latimer earned his first. By that time, Latimer was already at work for Edison, his third iconic inventor, after having assisted Bell and Maxim in prior years.

It's worth noting that Edison sued Woods twice for patent infringement – regarding railway telegraph designs – which was par for the course, as Edison was constantly litigating to extend his patent rights. Woods won both suits. And, completely in character, Edison then tried to hire Woods, as he had earlier hired Latimer. Woods declined. And, so, it did not come to pass that Edison employed both of the greatest African-American inventors of the nineteenth century.

There was the black Wall-Streeter, Jeremiah Hamilton, the richest person of color in the country when he died in 1875. Hamilton had been successful, and he was definitely well known, but was also widely disliked for his disreputable financial schemes.

Drawback and Drawing

To be first is, by definition, to be alone. The first are often celebrated. Bell and Edison certainly aimed to be and were. Maxim, too, aimed to be first. Though, after it became clear that his ambition would be thwarted by Edison, Maxim precipitously left for England, quitting the invention of our electric powered world for the invention of weaponry.

But the first are sometimes saddled with added scrutiny and skepticism. Such was Latimer's fate. In his career, not one of his colleagues were African American, let alone a son of escaped slaves. Rather they were European Americans, and generally they were raised in moderately or very prosperous families. Not one of his colleagues, in all likelihood, had ever encountered a black professional in commerce and industry, or had heard or read of one.

This must have been a source of discomfort for them, and Latimer must have sensed that, whether the discomfort was direct or disguised. Yet, for a goodly number of them, Latimer's skin color was recognized and then cast aside, remarkably, as their respect for Latimer the man grew.

Latimer likely was constantly aware of his aloneness, during his long days and nights at work. We know that Bell, the first of the three iconic inventors that Latimer assisted, was a prejudiced man. We know that while Maxim eagerly hired and quickly became dependent upon Latimer, he was amazed such a talent was a black man.

We know that the British electric lighting manufacturing workers Latimer supervised in London resented their new African American expert. And that the (likely aristocratic) bosses at British Maxim-Weston Electric Light Company resented him no less, as Latimer recorded in his journal:

> "The prevailing motif seemed to be humility of the workmen [now including Latimer] and the attitude that nothing I can do can repay you for permitting me to earn an honest living."

We know that even those colleagues back in America that admired him greatly, constantly called him "colored." Latimer wrote this (referring to himself in the third-person):

> "Now his color began to be a draw back to him. Every new workman who came into the office saw for the first time, a colored man making drawings; and as often as they came to work in the office they tried to pretend that he could not do their work. But he had had such long experience and was so well posted in all kinds of drawing that they soon were forced to acknowledge his exceeding ability which was far above the average at the time."

How Difficult It Must Have Been

Everyone faces challenges in their life, of course, no matter their circumstances. There are those that face more challenges than the rest of us. Among them, some who start out with seemingly every advantage. And certainly,

Lewis Latimer early in his career

those who start out with few advantages, or none, inevitably must face down challenges that would defeat all but the most determined.

Consider Lewis Latimer, born on September 4, 1848 in the industrial city of Chelsea, Massachusetts, directly across the Mystic River from Boston. An African American, this was a very real distinction since there were few blacks there or anywhere in the northeast corner of the country in the middle of the nineteenth century.

And, being born black in 1848 was by no means an advantage, even for the few that were born free. The presidential election, held two months after Latimer's birth, was the first to make abolition of slavery a legitimate national issue, though the Free Soil Party won just ten percent of the popular vote.

By this point in the nation's history, there had been precious few African Americans in any corner of the country who had achieved financial success or social standing of any sort. Among this very small number, most prominently there was Benjamin Banneker, the Maryland astronomer, James Derham, the New Orleans doctor, Alexander Lucius Twilight, the Vermont state legislator, and Frederick Douglass, the Massachusetts orator and author.

Douglass attended the Free Soil Party's convention that fall in 1848, which was a groundbreaking development for African Americans. He also served as secretary of the 1852 convention.

In attendance as well at the convention in 1848 was, notably, the poet Walt Whitman, the educational reformer Horace Mann, the future abolitionist leader in the U.S. Senate, Charles Sumner, and the future Supreme Court Chief Justice, Salmon Portland Chase.

It was Chase who finally reversed the high court's pro-slavery path under his predecessor Roger Taney. When Chase started his term, in December 1864 (while the Union gunboat that Lewis Latimer was serving on was readying for battle), his course became clear. Chief Justice Chase immediately admitted the first African American attorney to argue cases before his court, Dr. John Stewart Rock. Rock incidentally coined the phrase, "black is beautiful."

And, it was Charles Sumner who South Carolina congressman Preston Brooks nearly murdered, beating him with a cane – until it broke – on the floor of the U.S. Senate on May 26, 1856. A week earlier, Sumner had made his "Crime Against Kansas" speech, five hours of forceful rhetoric over two days against Slave Power (the political control over federal policies by slave owners), including for Brooks intolerable insults. The caning considerably increased northerners' indignation about southerners' strident statements, for the inviolable rights of slaveowners, and threatening secession from the national union.

Of the four great black men who had achieved success and standing by 1848, Banneker, Derham, Twilight and Douglass, two had been born in bondage. Derham had been freed by his slaver and Douglass had escaped slavery in Maryland for freedom in Massachusetts. In his speeches and writings, Douglass told of the realities of bondage, a visceral story that much of the nation had not heard before.

The Pearl and the Washington Riot

That fall of 1848, when Lewis Latimer was born, free blacks, enslaved blacks, and whites who advocated slavery's abolition were shaken and stirred to action by a dramatic development in Washington, D.C. In the spring, seventy-seven slaves made a daring attempt to flee to freedom by first sailing down the Potomac River and then turning northward in the Chesapeake Bay toward New Jersey aboard the schooner, The Pearl. When the wind didn't cooperate, a slaveholder posse was able to board and return the ship to Washington.

Not only were the recaptured slaves "sold down the river" to the extreme hardships of the deep south, but a mob of a thousand angered slavery supporters ravaged the city for the next three days. Two whites manning the ship were convicted and served years in prison, though in their trial they were vigorously defended by the educational reformer Horace Mann.

That fall, the freedom of two of the children, Emily and Mary Edmonson, was famously purchased making them celebrities; they soon joined Frederick Douglass and the abolitionist movement. The Pearl incident inspired the end of slave trading within the District of Columbia two years later and Harriet Beecher Stowe's extraordinarily influential book about slave life, "Uncle Tom's Cabin," four years later.

Slave, Free for Four Days, Prisoner, Free Forever

But in 1842, it was a full decade before the publication of Stowe's "Uncle Tom's Cabin." The abolitionist movement was still small and fragmented. Now, that was to change. George Latimer, desperate for freedom, determined to keep together his new family and have his first born be free born, came to be renown throughout the northeast and beyond as "the man who stole himself."

On October 4 of that year, George Latimer and his pregnant wife Rebecca made a daring escape from bondage, hiding beneath the forepeak of a ship in Norfolk that headed to Baltimore. They then crossed the border between slave and free states arriving in Philadelphia, with George – who had a relatively light skin color – pretending to be a slave master and Rebecca pretending to be his servant. After that, they traveled to Boston, assuming that settling down distant from slave states would minimize the risk of recapture by their slavers. They had now, on October 8, been free for four days.

But their luck was bad. George was spotted by an associate of his former slave owner, James B. Gray. The slaver travelled to Boston and then persuaded the sheriff to have his "property" jailed, invoking the Constitution's Fugitive Slave Clause and the Fugitive Slave Act of 1793, as if George was a thief that stole himself.

George did peaceably accept imprisonment, after having tasted freedom for just a few days. It was then that a second charge was rendered to the "offender." This time, he was charged as a deserter, from "service and labor," a creative characterization about someone fleeing their enslavement.

George Latimer wrote two months later:

"I have thought frequently about running away even when I was a little boy. I have frequently rolled up my sleeve, and asked – 'Can this flesh belong to any man as horses do?' Very few others would stay if they could get away. Some few, however, say they did wish to leave their masters. I expected if I was carried back, I would [be] beaten {sic} and whipped 39 lashes, and perhaps to be washing in pickle afterwards."

When George was imprisoned for stealing himself, it had only been six years since the precedent-setting Massachusetts Supreme Judicial Court case – Commonwealth versus Aves – for the freeing of slaves. Med, a six-year old slave girl who had been brought on a visit to Massachusetts by her New Orleans slaver, was declared free in August of 1836 upon entering Massachusetts, a state that had abolished slavery within its borders. The landmark opinion by Chief Justice Lemuel Shaw quickly became the precedent for similar actions in Connecticut, New York, Pennsylvania and Ohio.

It had only been five years since Frederick Douglass managed his daring escape that he would so thoroughly publicize during his illustrious career. And, it had been only four years since Douglass made it to the African American abolitionist David Ruggles in the Tribeca neighborhood in Manhattan, who hid the escapee and reunited him with his fiancée. Ruggles, who had opened the first African-American-owned bookstore, became legendary for outwitting the bounty hunters or "blackbirds" who wanted to capture free blacks and illegally sell them into southern slavery.

And, at the time that George Latimer was jailed, it had only been seven months since the U.S. Supreme Court handed down its decision in Prigg versus Pennsylvania. The high court held that the Fugitive Slave Act of 1793 prohibited Pennsylvania or any state from preventing the recapture of blacks to bring them back south into bondage, overturning the conviction of a slave catcher.

The Prigg versus Pennsylvania decision is also considered by historians to have increased the horrendous practice of kidnapping free blacks in the north and selling them to slavers in the south. This is the horror that was depicted in the 2013 movie, "12 Years a Slave," based on the true account of Solomon Northup in his 1853 memoir.

Just days after departing Norfolk, when George and Rebecca Latimer arrived in Boston, they landed in a starkly different world, for blacks particularly. Norfolk was the nation's thirty-sixth most populous city, with eleven thousand inhabitants. Boston was the nation's fifth most populous, nearly nine times larger, with ninety-three thousand.

Virginia, the state with the fourth highest population in 1840, had four hundred and eighty-one thousand blacks living within its borders, nearly forty-seven percent of the Old Dominion's population. Forty-nine thousand blacks were free and four hundred and thirty-two thousand were slaves. This comes out to be a ratio of one free black for every nine slaves.

Massachusetts, the state with the eighth highest population, had just nine thousand blacks living within its borders, a little bit over one percent of the Bay State's population. As few as they were, all of those nine thousand blacks were, of course, free.

According to that 1840 Census, there were only three hundred and eighty-six thousand free blacks anywhere in the U.S. The country's total population was seventeen million. So, free blacks were a rarity, only a little over two percent of all Americans. Black slaves weren't a rarity, of course, amounting to around fourteen percent of Americans. This means there were almost seven blacks in bondage in 1840, almost entirely within the southern states, for every one that was free, mostly within the northern states.

According to a 2015 Trinity College paper, "Slave or Free? White or Black? The Representation of George Latimer":

"His case, which became a benchmark in 1840s American history, roused New England antislavery advocates, recalibrated local and national understandings of slavery and freedom, and calcified divisions of state – Massachusetts versus Virginia – and nation – North versus South. George Latimer, the traditional narrative goes, helped send the nation down the divided path to civil war."

The month-long legal and political standoff over George Latimer's freedom concluded when abolitionist Dr. Henry Bowditch – a co-editor of the new thrice-weekly "Latimer Journal and North Star" – purchased Latimer's freedom from the slaver Gray for six hundred and fifty dollars. Well, almost. Latimer was released but Bowditch dithered about paying the slaver. The Reverend Samuel Caldwell of the Tremont Temple Baptist Church didn't want to chance it and handed Gray four hundred dollars, ending the matter.

George Latimer, now free, decided to help other fugitive slaves avoid what had happened to him. He put together so-called Latimer Petitions urging legislation protecting fugitive slaves from recapture. Over a hundred thousand signatures were presented to the U.S. Congress by Congressman John Quincy Adams, the former President, but to no avail.

Though the Massachusetts legislature did act, passing the state's Personal Liberty Law in March of 1843, making it illegal for state officials to help recapture runaways. The legislation, which was commonly known as the "Latimer Law," was written about by the poet John Greenleaf Whittier:

"No slave-hunt in our borders, – no pirate on our strand!
No fetters in the Bay State, – no slave upon our land!"

Despite his celebrity and work in the abolitionist movement, George was later a man hounded into hiding, after fifteen years as a free man. He was justifiably fearful of being brought back into southern slavery when the U.S. Supreme Court infamously decided the Dred Scott versus Sandford case. At the time of this fateful ruling, the youngest of his four children, Lewis Latimer, hadn't yet reached his ninth birthday.

Education at Phillips Grammar School Cut Short

Lewis Latimer consequently had to leave behind his schooling at the age of ten, making it to the fifth grade at Boston's Phillips Grammar School. He had been such a good student that he skipped a grade. This school on Beacon Hill, considered one of the best in Boston, was as well one of the first in Boston to enroll black children just three years prior, soon after the Massachusetts legislature integrated the city's schools.

Phillips Grammar School was named for the first mayor of Boston, John Phillips. This man was not only Boston's first mayor, inaugurated at Faneuil Hall on May 1, 1822, when that city had a population of forty-five thousand. John Phillips was also the father of one of the leading abolitionists in the years leading up to the Civil War, Wendell Phillips.

Wendell Phillips was squarely in the forefront of the battle against George Latimer's recapture by the Virginia slave owner in 1842, under the Fugitive Slave Law that the nation's founders very unfortunately enacted into law back in 1793. He joined the burgeoning abolitionist movement and the American Anti-Slavery Society after witnessing the near lynching of William Lloyd Garrison, publisher of The Liberator, the leading abolitionist newspaper, in the fall of 1835.

As told fifty-three years later by a Wendell Phillips biographer:

"The rioters had discovered his [Garrison's] hiding place, and, amid yells which were heard afar off, dragged him to a window, and were about to throw him out, when the conscience of one of them caused him to interfere. Then they drew him back, and coiled a rope around his body, evidently with the intention of dragging him through the streets of Boston."

Wendell Phillips later pushed the Massachusetts legislature to pass the Personal Liberty Law to prohibit slave recaptures within the state. And, he pushed for an amendment to the U.S. Constitution to prohibit the practice nationally. And, he even advocated that the state secede from the Union if this change couldn't pass, ironic given the southern states' secession in 1861.

When Wendell Phillips passed away in 1884, the great Frederick Douglass said in his eulogy at the Phillips funeral:

"Not only the cruelty and wickedness of slavery, but its superlative meanness, stirred his soul and kindled his moral indignation. He gave no quarter to its defenders at any point, but poured the living coals of truth, and his boundless wealth of scorn and execration, upon the system and the men who upheld it."

There's no question that both John and Wendell Phillips knew that little Lewis was the son of the man whose freedom they championed in the decade before. And, it's likely this studious young man received a very good education while at Phillips Grammar School. That is, before the Supreme Court's Dred Scott versus Sandford decision derailed all that, forcing Lewis' father George Latimer into hiding, and compelling Lewis to go to work to make a living at the age of ten.

After Having to Leave Behind Phillips Grammar

Lewis Latimer's journal as a child, written in the third person, tells us that: "his two brothers were sent to a state institution then known as the Farm School [for vocational training], from where they were bound out [as apprentices]. George was sent to a farmer and William to a hotel keeper in Springfield. Margaret, Lewis's sister, was taken by a friend and Lewis remained in his mother's home until she got the chance to go to sea as a stewardess … [and] arranged to send him to the Farm School."

As a pre-teen, he worked at a series of odd jobs, waiting on tables, housework for a family in Roxbury, and delivering Garrison's abolitionist newspaper, The Liberator. Garrison had started printing this newspaper at the dawn of the abolitionist movement in the early eighteen-thirties, well before George Latimer and even Frederick Douglass had fled southern slavery.

It was at the end of the eighteen-twenties, in the fall of 1829, that David Walker, a free black living in Boston, published "An Appeal to the Coloured Citizens of the World." The book's impact was enormous. In 1831, Garrison's newspaper started printing. That same year, an unprecedented resistance of some seventy enslaved and free blacks near the southern border of Virginia, Nat Turner's rebellion, resulted in much bloodshed on both sides and backlash by whites throughout the south. Two years later, Great Britain passed the Slavery Abolition Act, and the American Anti-Slavery Society organized.

Gunboat Seaman at Howlett's House Batteries

Around the beginning of the Civil War, twelve-year old Lewis Latimer landed a position in a professional office, that of the prominent Boston lawyer Isaac Hull Wright, as an office boy. Perhaps the young man was able there to resume some of the intellectual development that he had started years earlier at Phillips Grammar School. That Wright brought Latimer into his practice makes one think that the young man was already showing some promise.

We can also speculate that Wright might have had a special interest in George Latimer's youngest son Lewis. Was Isaac Wright related to Elizur Wright, a leading abolitionist and member of the Boston Vigilance Committee that defended George against a forced return to southern slavery? Elizur did have nine siblings, and Isaac had seven, so it's possible. In any case, Elizur is best remembered as a mathematician and the "father of life insurance and insurance regulation."

In the middle of the Civil War, when Latimer was fifteen, he left Wright's employ and enlisted in the U.S. Navy as a landsman on the U.S.S. Massasoit. His older brothers George and William were already fighting for the Union,

**USS Massasoit, the steam side-wheel gunboat
Lewis Latimer served on during the Civil War**

George in the Twenty-ninth Connecticut Army Regiment (that state's first African American force), and William in the Navy. Soon Latimer would find himself in the heat of battle for the national union and its creed for freedom.

Of the seventeen thousand and six hundred black men who served in the Navy during the entire course of the Civil War, eighty-two percent were rated as a landsman – the lowest rating and below seaman – commonly called "boys." They were typically assigned the menial unskilled work aboard a ship.

A large majority of these sailors were former slaves who escaped from bondage during the chaos of the war, commonly called "contrabands" (as opposed to "freeborn" like Lewis Latimer). Eight percent were rated as cooks and stewards, which earned these men premium pay and technically the title of petty officer, though they were generally treated as servants. In the third quarter of 1864 for example, the Navy had a total of just thirteen blacks rated as bona fide "petty officers of the line."

The two hundred foot double-ender sidewheel Sassacus Class gunboat, displacing nearly a thousand tons and manned by a complement of about a hundred fifty officers and crew, finally got into action a year later, in the late summer of 1864. Named after the chief of the Wampanoag Indians of New England, who assisted the Plymouth Colony but fathered King Philip who warred with the colonists, the U.S.S. Massasoit first patrolled the coast of New England in search of Confederate raiders.

Then the heavily-armed gunboat, captained by the distinguished Commander Richard T. Renshaw, joined the North Atlantic Blockading Squadron of Rear Admiral David D. Porter. The U.S.S. Massasoit then served picket duty in the James River in Virginia, from where Latimer's father has escaped slavery twenty-two years earlier.

Most notably, it then dueled Confederate batteries at the strategic point of Howlett's House on January 24, 1865. General U.S. Grant's army captured Petersburg and Richmond in just over two months.

The report of the U.S.S. Massasoit said this about the fight at Howlett's House:

"At 10:12 beat to quarters and prepared the ship for action. At 10:35 opened fire upon the swamp and Howlett house batteries. At 11:55 a.m. ceased firing ... Being for the greater part of the time very nearly abreast of the Crow's Nest battery, of which the enemy have very accurate range, we were struck several times by shot and shell, but sustained no serious injury. Too much credit can not be given to the officers and crew for the manner in which they conducted themselves during the action. It being the first action the crew ever participated in, they deserve special commendation, acting, as they did, like veterans. Our list of wounded amounts to five …"

In listing the five wounded, the surgeon wrote that three of the five were landsmen, which is what Lewis Latimer was on the ship, of which two were in serious condition.

The U.S.S. Massasoit was decommissioned on the twenty-seventh of June, following the war's end. On the third of July, less than three months after the Confederacy's Army of Northern Virginia surrendered at Appomattox Courthouse, Latimer was honorably discharged from the Navy.

Without prospects, with persistence

Latimer remained extremely patriotic throughout his life, and actively participated as an officer of the veterans group, the Grand Army of the Republic, likely a rarity for an African-American. But now, at the end of the Civil War, Latimer was seventeen years old, without prospects.

As Latimer recalled (in third person as usual):

"He went from place to place … finally a colored girl who took care of the office of some lady copyists … was asked to recommend a colored boy as office boy, one 'with a taste for drawing.' [He] got the place at three dollars a week [at Crosby and Gould, a Boston patent law firm].

He believed then that whatever a man knew he had put in a book, so when he saw the [draughts] man making drawings he watched to find out what tools he used, then went to a second hand book store and got a book on drawing and soon had a set of drawing instruments.

He then looked over the draughtsman's shoulder to see how he used his instruments, and practiced with them at home until he felt thoroughly master of them, then one day he asked the draughtsman to let him do some drawing for him, the man laughed at him but finally consented to look at what he could do … and to his surprise found that Lewis was a real draughtsman …

One day the boss saw him at work and was so pleased that he let him work everyday and gradually raised his wages so that from three dollars when he went to work he rose in eleven years to twenty dollars a week."

Latimer eventually rose to chief draftsman at Crosby and Gould and worked there for eleven years. Near the end of this period, and when the firm's leadership was changing, Latimer started working with a curious professor obsessive about sound and hearing.

Chapter Two

Bell Completes the Telephone Patent Application, with Latimer

Aren't You George Latimer's Son?

It's Valentine's Day. The year is 1876, the country's centennial. A Boston University professor, specializing in vocal physiology and elocution, Alexander Graham Bell, orders his lawyer to rush an application to the U.S. Patent and Trademark Office. Every hour counts. Indeed, every minute counts. For Bell knows that Elisha Gray, an accomplished electrical engineer and professor of dynamic electricity at Oberlin College (who incidentally developed the first music synthesizer), has been preparing an application for the very same invention. Bell knows that the telephone will revolutionize society. And he knows that its inventor, be that Gray or himself, will become forever famous.

Lewis Latimer in the middle of his career

That momentous fourteenth of February fell on a Monday. It had been a frantic weekend. Bell learned just three days earlier, on Friday the eleventh, that Gray had readied his patent application. Its filing was imminent.

Until that Friday, Gray's work on the telephone was a well-kept secret. The source of his funding for inventions and patents was a dentist, Dr. Samuel White, who was wealthy from producing porcelain teeth. The dentist wants Gray to focus on multiplexing the telegraph, sending multiple messages on a single wire, in order to drive down the cost of telegraphy. But Gray knows that path would be fruitless. The telephone's emergence will wipe out telegraphy.

So, for Bell, this weekend was make-or-break. Bell, twenty-nine and just six years removed from coming to North America (emigrating to Canada from Scotland), Thomas Watson, just twenty-two, who constructed Bell's electrical devices, and Lewis Latimer, twenty-eight, the patent expert and draftsman who had been brought in to persuade the Patent Office, worked flat out on the twelfth and thirteenth of February.

Lewis Latimer? We all know about Alexander Graham Bell. His place in history has been large and long-lived. The Bell System of companies dominated the telephone industry for its first hundred years plus and was commonly called Ma Bell. Thomas Watson, we know him too, as Bell's sidekick. More on him below. But, Lewis Latimer? How does Latimer fit into the story of the telephone's invention?

The Bell application needed to beat Gray's. It had to win the race to the Patent Office, first of all. And then, of course, it had to convince the clerks there that it was Bell that had invented the telephone, and that the device it described was distinct from any and all devices of a similar nature heretofore patented.

Latimer's memoirs recalled this time:

> "I was obliged to stay at the office until after nine P.M. when he [Bell] was free from his night classes, to get my instructions from him, as to how I was to make the drawings for the application for a patent upon the telephone."

Bell recalled that he "had done his best work late at night, when all was still and he could focus his thoughts," according to Bell biographer Robert V. Bruce. His teaching schedule at Boston University, filled with evening classes, necessitated the late nights that Latimer and Bell describe.

Colored Office Boy Masters Patents

The Constitution of the United States, Article I, Section 8, established patents as a core principle of the American economy. Congress had subsequently specified over the years leading up to that historic weekend in 1876 the ground rules that governed how the application for a telephone patent would fare.

A successful patent, which secured for the inventor a seventeen-year monopoly, must be for a device that was "not before known or used." The application must be printed. And it must, critically, include black and white drawings depicting the device. That Latimer was an expert draftsman for patent applications, and that he was by then an expert in wording applications, was invaluable to Bell on that weekend before Valentine's Day 1876.

But Latimer, still employed by Crosby and Gould at the time, was but one of many expert draftsmen in Boston. Crosby and Gould certainly prized his work and apparently didn't care much or at all about the color of his skin; although the firm originally sought to hire a "colored office boy."

By 1876, Latimer had one patent under his belt already. The successful patent application, at age twenty-six, in collaboration with a Charles Warren Brown, for a significant improvement to the railroad car toilet, was witnessed by Latimer's boss Francis Gould.

Crosby and Gould was located one block from Bell's laboratory. Somehow, Bell and Latimer met. What caused them to meet has not been recorded. But it wouldn't be at all surprising that the man who later famously said, "Watson, come here, I need you," asked upon first meeting Latimer, "you're George Latimer's son, aren't you?"

All his life, up to that chance meeting with Bell, Lewis Latimer was undoubtedly constantly reminded of his famous father, George Latimer. In Boston, the father was a celebrity and so must have been his youngest son, Lewis.

Latimer's Father George Wasn't and Was Present

In 1876, George Latimer was fifty-seven years old and a free man for thirty-four years, since the landmark resistance movement when the abusive slave owner James Gray traveled to Boston to return "his property" back to Virginia. Abolitionists and many northerners had been outraged by this first attempt to recapture escaped slaves from the free states, and they rallied to George's ultimately successful cause to remain free.

George had remained as a prominent voice in the abolitionist movement for a few years and then settled down as a paper-hanger near Boston, in Lynn, Massachusetts. That is, until the U.S. Supreme Court's notorious Dred Scott Decision when George's freedom was again threatened. Chief Justice Roger Taney, on behalf of the Court's seven-to-two majority, wrote that African Americans couldn't be citizens since they have: "… been regarded as beings of an inferior order … and so far inferior that they had no rights which the white man was bound to respect." Taney also said that the government's role in slavery was: "… the power coupled with the duty of guarding and protecting the [slave] owner in his rights." Little wonder that George Latimer, lacking any legal documentation of his freedom, and as one of the most famous runaways, ran a second time so he would be impossible for slave catchers to find.

He remained anonymous though never far from his family and abolitionist friends such as John W. Hutchinson. George Latimer wrote this in 1893, three years before he passed away:

"The [Hutchinson] family all did noble work for the cause of the slave. I am now in my seventy-fourth year. For forty-five years I pursued the trade of a paperhanger in Lynn. My days in Virginia seem like a dream to me. I am glad to add these few words in recognition of the services to liberty of the Hutchinson Family, and to speak again my sense of gratitude to those who with them aroused the North in an agitation that made freedom possible for me and mine."

The next year, 1894, Frederick Douglass, the black community's senior statesman, and George's youngest son Lewis Latimer, the black community's foremost man of commerce, corresponded. Douglas wrote:

"It is fifty two years since I first saw your father and mother in Boston. You can hardly imagine the excitement the attempts to recapture them caused in Boston. It was a new experience for the Abolitionists and they improved it to the full extent of which it was capable."

Watson, I Want You

Watson was a young tinkerer who assembled Bell's phone. Watson's fame lives on. Bell often recounted that first phone conversation, during his demonstrations promoting telephony, in which he had said, "Watson, come here, I want you." There was to be more than fame in Watson's future, but fortune as well. Bell gave Watson a share of the skyrocketing telephone business, who later parlayed that to become a successful shipbuilder.

As for Latimer, there's no record of Bell crediting him, let alone richly rewarding him. Yet, there would have been no patent application on that Valentine's Day, by Bell, without this first hidden figure. Without Latimer, Bell would not have beaten Gray to the Patent Office. Gray rather than Bell would have been anointed as the telephone's inventor.

Why do we only know a few bare facts suggesting Latimer's role? Perhaps it's due to Bell's oversized ego, and the inventor's aim to absorb all the adulation. Latimer, throughout his career, was a serial supporter of great men – such as Bell, and later Maxim and Edison – who embraced exaggerated accounts of their roles in civilization's progress with a sharp eye on their legacies.

Latimer was modest by nature. Perhaps Bell considered Latimer's role – putting together an artful and persuasive patent – of secondary importance. But just perhaps, since Latimer was African American, Bell felt he couldn't or wouldn't publicly recognize Latimer's genius and decisive contribution to their success.

Bell was an early and very active supporter of the eugenics movement – which continued throughout his life – that gained momentum in the late nineteenth century and early twentieth century and culminated with the atrocities of Adolf Hitler and the Nazis. Indeed, Bell was the honorary president of the Second International Conference on Eugenics in 1921, just two years before Hitler started writing Mein Kampf in a German prison following the Beer Hall Putsch.

The telephone's inventor was concerned about "undesirable ethnical elements" and wanted legislation to encourage the "evolution of a higher and nobler type of man in America," including immigration restrictions and compulsory sterilization of people he deemed "a defective variety of the human race." Which makes one wonder how Bell viewed Latimer, who he knew to be an extremely accomplished man, but not a northern European like the Scottish-born Bell.

Reconstruction Retrenched

The year was 1876 when Latimer worked with Bell into the night to craft a compelling patent application and do so before Bell's competitor could. The centennial year was not just right in the middle of an incredible surge in invention. It was as well a time of a terrible transformation in civil society. Historians of the period of segregation mark 1876 as the year the Jim Crow culture took hold in the south and beyond.

Just eleven years had passed since the Confederacy collapsed and the Civil War ended. African Americans were enjoying some of the freedoms accorded other Americans for the first time, during the decade since the surrender at Appomattox Courthouse. But things really started going downhill after the Panic of 1873, which remained ruinous past the time of Bell's and Latimer's collaboration.

Public support for Reconstruction, the policies that promoted some degree of racial equality in the south, dwindled during the eighteen-seventies. This only accelerated during the Panic years, which devastated the south especially, forcing defaulting landowners off their farms and plummeting wages for indebted workers. The Democrats, who had long wanted to dismantle Reconstruction, won control in 1874 of the House of Representatives from the Republicans, demoralized by the corruption of President Ulysses Grant's second term and idealism's frustrations. This Democrat majority was the first since the secession of the southern states that started the Civil War.

Racism raged in the north too. Increasingly, African Americans were blamed for Reconstruction's lingering and growing problems particularly the revival of violence by Confederate veterans. Bell, Latimer and all Americans in the mid-1880s would have read in their dailies about the founding of the domestic terrorist groups, the White League in Louisiana and Red Shirts in Mississippi and the Carolinas. These militias operated in the open and brazenly to suppress African Americans and reconstitute Democrat and white supremacy throughout the southern states as documented by the great political cartoonist Thomas Nast in Harper's Weekly, among others.

And, the Supreme Court started retrenching on civil rights, first in the Slaughterhouse Cases of 1873, which pruned away the power of the Fourteenth Amendment over state laws violating due process and equal protection. And then most notoriously in United States versus Cruikshank in 1876. The landmark case was argued before the Court only a few months prior to the telephone patent application and was decided only a few weeks after the application.

This one judicial decision really reversed the civil rights progress that had been achieved since the Fourteenth Amendment became law eight years earlier, virtually ensuring segregation and violence against African-Americans would continue for nearly the next hundred years. The Court held that the federal government could not take enforcement action against individuals, or against states, that deprive the rights of other individuals.

As did an armed white Democrat militia on Easter Sunday in 1873, in Colfax, Louisiana, in the Colfax massacre. As many as two hundred and eighty African Americans were mercilessly murdered, most of them following their surrender. The Court overturned the conviction of three white men who murdered a hundred black men.

In doing so, the Court presided by Chief Justice Morrison Waite, who believed Reconstruction's laws and Constitutional amendments should be narrowly interpreted, dissolved the effectiveness of Congress' Enforcement Act of 1870 meant to curb Ku Klux Klan violence. Chief Justice Waite actually concluded, "We may suspect that race was the cause of the hostility but it is not so averred."

Within a year of the telephone's patent, Reconstruction was done in by the Compromise of 1877. The Republican candidate for President cut a deal with the Democrat who either narrowly lost or narrowly won the election's electoral college. Rutherford Hayes, the Republican, got the Presidency. The Democrats got the end of Reconstruction and the federal troop presence in the south that went along with it. Biracial state and local governance in the south was soon dispatched and black participation in elections effectively disappeared.

The Chicago Tribune wrote: "The long controversy over the black man seems to have reached a finality." The Nation wrote: "The negro will disappear from the field of national politics. Henceforth, the nation, as a nation, will have nothing more to do with him."

Latimer's First Big Break

Up until Latimer's work with Bell in 1876 and in the eighteen-eighties and eighteen-nineties with Hiram Maxim and Thomas Edison, he was best known as the son of George Latimer, the famous runaway slave. The most prominent abolitionists of the eighteen-forties, including former President

John Quincy Adams and William Lloyd Garrison, had helped George Latimer prevent the slave owner from returning him to Virginia in 1842.

One of those prominent abolitionists was William Francis Channing. He was the son of the foremost Unitarian theologian William Ellery Channing who had died that same year.

William Francis Channing was so incensed by the slave owner's intentions that he immediately co-founded the Latimer Journal, which went on to become a widely-read abolitionist newspaper. Then, twenty-four years passed. Channing, who in the interim had co-invented the first citywide electric fire alarm system (using the new technology of telegraphy), started working on the telephone's development with, guess who, Alexander Graham Bell.

It was Channing, collaborating with John Pierce, a professor of chemistry at Brown University, who came up with the handset. Bell's telephone was actually a bulky box.

Did Lewis Latimer and Channing – a man who had worked so fervently for the freedom of Latimer's father in the eighteen-forties – know they were both working with Bell in the eighteen-seventies on the invention that would transform how the world communicates? They must have known this. They must have met during this time. Speculating further, is it because of their relationship that Latimer – the talented but young African American patent specialist – came to work for Bell in the inventor's time of greatest need?

It's a question we cannot answer definitively. However, there's another interesting connection between Latimer and Channing. Later in Latimer's life, he became very active in the Unitarian church. He helped lead one in his Flushing neighborhood of Queens, New York with a predominantly white congregation. Not only was William Francis Channing the son of the foremost Unitarian theologian of his time, but his cousin William Henry Channing was well-known as a Unitarian clergyman.

Myth and Reality of Late Nineteenth Century Invention

We cannot say for sure how Bell and Latimer came to collaborate. Though, we can conclude that Bell and later Hiram Maxim and Thomas Edison depended upon the remarkable Lewis Latimer as they invented the modern world. The three inventors all depended on Latimer, notwithstanding the prevailing opinions of the late nineteenth century about African Americans, that they weren't and couldn't be significant contributors to the Second Industrial Revolution.

Considering the biases Latimer faced every day, he must have been very special, to have been given such responsibilities and respect – albeit privately – by the most celebrated inventors. That circumstantial evidence is clear. Bell, Maxim and Edison apparently couldn't do without him.

Who Gets the Credit?

It seems like everybody who was anybody in late nineteenth century invention knew everybody. Alexander Graham Bell, the telephone's inventor who depended upon Lewis Latimer's skill in the patenting of inventions, met Helen Keller in 1886. What happened next was famously dramatized by the hit 1962 movie "The Miracle Worker" starring Patty Duke and Anne Bancroft. Bell soon sent Anne Sullivan to Keller's home to help the young blind and deaf girl communicate. Keller went on to a productive life, graduating Radcliffe College in 1904, the first blind and deaf person to do so.

Why do we bring this up? Because the iconic Mark Twain wrote an insightful letter to Keller while she was attending Radcliffe, on the nature of innovation. Keller had overcome charges of plagiarism years earlier, concerning a short story she wrote. Twain was still ticked off about the false charges.

In the letter, Twain complained about our need to anoint a single inventor of creative works, so eloquently as was his nature:

"Oh, dear me, how unspeakably funny and owlishly idiotic and grotesque was that 'plagiarism' farce! As if there was much of anything in any human utterance, oral or written, except plagiarism!

The kernel, the soul – let us go further and say the substance, the bulk, the actual and valuable material of all human utterances – is plagiarism. For substantially all ideas are second-hand, consciously and unconsciously drawn from a million outside sources, and daily used by the garnerer with a pride and satisfaction born of the superstition that he originated them; whereas there is not a rag of originality about them anywhere except a little discoloration they get from his mental and moral calibre and his temperament, and which is revealed in characteristics of phrasing.

When a great orator makes a great speech you are listening to ten centuries and ten thousand men – but we call it his speech, and really some exceedingly small portion of it is his. But not enough to signify. It is merely a Waterloo. It is Wellington's battle, in some degree, and we call it his; but there are others that contributed.

It takes a thousand men to invent a telegraph, or a steam engine, or a phonograph, or a telephone or any other important thing – and the last man gets the credit and we forget the others. He added his little mite – that is all he did.

These object lessons should teach us that ninety-nine parts of all things that proceed from the intellect are plagiarisms, pure and simple; and the lesson ought to make us modest. But nothing can do that."

Not surprisingly, Twain knew both Edison and his rival Nikola Tesla, and the war of currents over creative credit. Also of relevance to Latimer's life, Twain authored a searing satire about slavery and racism, "Pudd'nhead Wilson, in 1894, two years before the notorious U.S. Supreme Court decision in Plessy versus Ferguson. Latimer had a senior role in Edison General Electric's Law Department at the time.

One of the lessons of the extraordinary 2016 movie "Hidden Figures," and the book it was based on by Margot Lee Shetterly, was that astronaut John Glenn didn't win the space race in the nineteen-sixties on his own, notwithstanding Glenn's grit and grace. Neither did the Space Task Group headed by Al Harrison, or any other individual or small group at NASA. Rather it was a glorious team effort of the nation's brightest and most dedicated scientists and engineers, including of course three remarkable African American women, Katherine Johnson, Mary Jackson and Dorothy Vaughn. Their critical contributions were all the more remarkable given the trying racial barriers they faced, and that they overcame.

Sounds like the story of Lewis Latimer, does it not? The first human figure made critical contributions to the telephone's and electric light's invention, accomplishments that were hardly those of Alexander Graham Bell and Thomas Edison alone. And, just as we all think of Bell and Edison when these great inventions are mentioned, and not Lewis Latimer and other faceless contributors, we typically think of Glenn when the space race comes up in conversation. But, it must be said that, as "Hidden Figures" shows, Glenn was nothing like Bell and Edison. The courageous astronaut clearly recognized the brilliance of the black geniuses on his team.

Chapter Three

Maxim Competes with Edison, with Latimer's Filament

He's Colored

Latimer had played that pivotal role in one of history's greatest inventions, the telephone. But by the fall of 1879, three years later, Latimer is just a paper hanger in Bridgeport, Connecticut. He had moved his family to the South End there – a melting pot neighborhood of Irish, Hungarians, African Americans, etc. – near where his sister Margaret and her husband lived, in the hope his prospects might improve in this renowned center of late nineteenth century innovation.

Just after the extraordinary experience with Bell, and after leaving the employ of what was now called Crosby and Gregory, Latimer began a new section of his journal, which he entitled Electrical Recollections. From that point on, he was an electricity man.

Latimer had stayed in Boston for a couple more years, working first for another patent lawyer, Joseph Adams, and then at Esterbrook Iron Foundry. But Bridgeport and the many opportunities there beckoned.

Of Bridgeport, Latimer wrote that it was:

"… a perfect hornets' nest of industries. The place is perfectly alive with inventors and it would be next to impossible to throw a stone into any company of men … without hitting one."

Oddly, Bridgeport's mayor in the years immediately before, until 1876, had been none other than Phineas Taylor Barnum. That's right, it was P.T. Barnum who said, "there's a sucker born every minute." By the time Latimer arrived, Barnum had abandoned politics and focused his energies on promoting his Barnum & Bailey Circus.

Fortunately, aside from paper hanging, Latimer had a side gig at a local business, Follansbee Machine Shop, in his chosen profession of draftsman. And who would walk into that machine shop but Hiram Maxim, the serial if eccentric inventor. Yes, that's right, this is the same man who five years later invents the machine gun, for which Maxim is best known, and is most reviled. The machine gun was first used in battle less than a decade later in what is now Zimbabwe, when British colonial police killed fifteen hundred Ndebele warriors while losing four of their own force; with but five of the guns Maxim developed.

Maxim over the years secured patents for an odd collection of innovations, including the hair-curling iron and the fire sprinkler. A serial bigamist, marrying three women in his lifetime without divorcing any, apparently conceived of and was the first to perform the magic trick of sawing someone in half, in the first instance a parlor maid before an audience at his London home in 1910.

The Maxims were quite a family. In later years, Hudson Maxim, Hiram's brother, invented smokeless gunpowder. Though, since the patent was issued to H. Maxim, Hiram and Hudson fought over the rights and remained distant from then on. And then there's Hiram Percy Maxim, Hiram's son, who invented the firearm silencer.

Maxim spots Latimer in Follansbee Machine Shop in February 1880 and is amazed and delighted, by Latimer's standout skill as an industrial draftsman, and indeed as a "colored" draftsman. Maxim immediately hires Latimer, as Maxim's general assistant as well as a draftsman.

Hired on the Spot

Latimer wrote in his diary, "Within a week from the time we first met I was installed in Mr. Maxim's office busily following my vocation of mechanical draughtsman, and acquainting myself in every branch of incandescent light construction and operation."

It's fateful that the eclectic Maxim is, at this time, into electric lighting. Indeed, his United States Electric Lighting Company is Thomas Edison's top competitor in this new field that is about to explode. By the fall of 1880, only two firms are marketing incandescent lighting systems, Maxim's company and Edison's. Maxim actually has the edge on Edison. Maxim's filaments last longer, in part due to Latimer's inventiveness. "My lamps gave fully twice as much light for the power consumed as Edison's original lamps," said Maxim.

Maxim resented Edison's salesmanship of what in our time might be called vaporware, and he once remarked, "Every time I put up a light a crowd would gather, everyone asking, 'Is it Edison's?' As Edison had never made a lamp up to that time, I was annoyed and told [U.S. Lighting Company's founder Spencer D.] Schuyler that the next time anyone said that I would kill him on the spot."

The New York Times, in an editorial published in November of 1879, on the eve of Edison's historic invention announcement, wrote this:

"The perfection of Mr. Edison's electric light has been trumpeted so many times that the distinguished inventor may find it reasonable to excuse a little skepticism on the part of the public and a very considerable amount from expert electricians. As long ago as last June it was whispered about that the month of July would not pass without a wonderful and convincing exhibition of Mr. Edison's light that would set gas shares [of companies fueling gas lighting] tumbling. July, August, September and October went by and now it is announced that an exhibition will soon be given … but no date is assigned."

A Better Filament

Latimer submitted his patent application, "The Process for Manufacturing Carbons," on February 19, 1881. It had been only one year earlier that Thomas Edison's senior engineer (his "mathematician") published the first exposition of the light bulb invention in a Scribner's article, "Edison's Electric Light." It took eleven months for Latimer to receive the patent. But then he was expected to assign the patent to the U.S. Electric Lighting Company. The profits went to the company rather than to Latimer.

It cannot be overstated how critically important to Edison, Maxim, Latimer and all those others pursuing the perfection and patenting of incandescent electric lighting was the improvement of the filament, its orientation and attachment within a light bulb and its mass manufacturing. Edison devoted much of his time in this pursuit, as did Latimer.

While waiting for that patent, Latimer and Nichols earned themselves another patent, for an improved incandescent lamp. This Latimer light bulb and its unique light socket was cited as a leading lamp by one of Thomas Edison's closest associates in those days, William Joseph Hammer, who joined Edison in December 1879 and became his Chief Engineer just months later.

But Maxim referred to Latimer's lamp, quite characteristically, as the "Maxim electric lamp." And, arrogantly, though well within his authority to do so, Maxim had Latimer's filaments shaped into an M, this being the first letter of Hiram's last name. Latimer wrote years later that Maxim was "… exceedingly jealous of anything in the nature of inventive ability being displayed by any of the workman."

A contemporary and colleague of Maxim was Professor William Edward Sawyer. He had successfully defended his incandescent patents against lawsuits brought by Thomas Edison through much of the eighteen-eighties. And, his lamps were used by George Westinghouse to illuminate the historic 1893 World's Columbian Exposition in Chicago. Sawyer said this about Maxim:

> "I know Mr. Maxim very well, and while he is beyond doubt one of the best mechanical engineers in this country, I have no hesitation in saying that in his last attempt at electric lighting he has made a wholesale appropriation [taking or making use of without permission] of other people's property."

The National Academy of Sciences met in November of 1880 at which Professor Henry Morton, founder and president of the prestigious Stevens Institute of Technology, stated that the filament in the Maxim electric lamp was more durable and practical than what he had seen in Thomas Edison's factory. Maxim and Edison then battled in the courts as to who had invented what first and patent rights. Edison brought suit three times between February (when Latimer submitted his patent application on filament manufacturing) and August of 1881, with Maxim coming out on top in every instance at each appeal.

As the elite group, the Edison Pioneers, wrote, upon Latimer's passing on December 11, 1928:

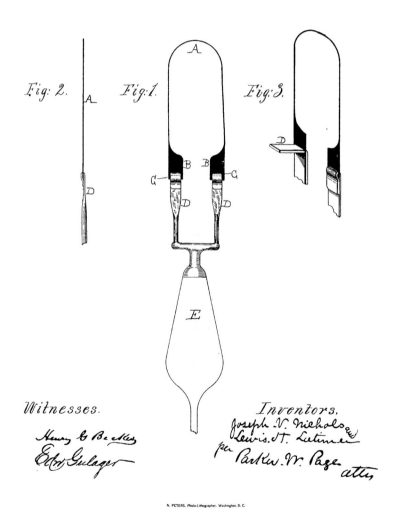

Lewis Latimer's 1881 electric lamp patent, with Joseph V. Nichols

"It was while in this employ [for Hiram Maxim at the U.S. Electric Lighting Company], that Mr. Latimer successfully produced a method of making carbon filaments for the Maxim electric incandescent lamp, which he patented. His keen perception of the possibilities of the electric light and kindred industries resulted in his being the author of several other inventions. He assisted in installing and placing in operation some of the first "Maxim" incandescent electric light plants in New York City, Philadelphia and Canada for the United States Electric Lighting Company, and supervised the production of the carbon filaments employed therein, such as the Equitable Building, Fiske & Hatch, Caswell & Massey's, and the Union League Club of New York City, as well as the offices of the Philadelphia 'Ledger' in Philadelphia."

Latimer is Made Leader

Latimer swiftly moved up the ladder. At the time, Bridgeport, Connecticut, the original home of the company's incandescent lighting department, was the Silicon Valley of technological innovation. Before long, Latimer became an active member of the Bridgeport Scientific Society, most likely the sole professional of color at their gatherings, and presented a paper there entitled "Practical Relation of Art to Science." He was also a frequent author of scholarly articles including "The Progress of Invention."

The company's factory moved to New York City in June of 1880, and Latimer and his family with it. Then, in the fall of 1880, Maxim, Latimer and company installed the very first commercial incandescent lighting system, ahead of Edison and everyone else. It was put into the building that housed the Equitable Life Insurance Company (that had financed the founding of the U.S. Electric Lighting Company).

Edison does get the credit for installing incandescent lighting before this. But this was on a steamship, the Columbia, owned by the wealthy stockholder Henry Villard (who helped finance Edison Electric Light Company). Edison's installation took place in the spring of 1880, a few months before Maxim's achievement. The race between Edison and Maxim was on.

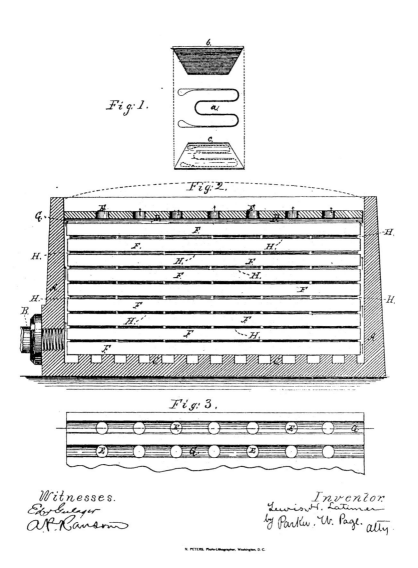

(No.Model.)

L. H. LATIMER.

PROCESS OF MANUFACTURING CARBONS.

No. 252,386.   Patented Jan. 17, 1882.

Fig. 1.

Fig. 2.

Fig. 3.

Witnesses.   Inventor.

N. PETERS. Photo-Lithographer, Washington, D. C.

Lewis Latimer's 1882 process of manufacturing carbons patent

The Boss is Black

The next summer, in 1881, Maxim promotes Latimer to superintendent of the incandescent lighting department, in effect, the company's chief electrical engineer, supervising forty men. That's forty men who undoubtedly knew it was unique that their thirty-three year old leader is an African American. No one had ever heard of such a thing.

The U.S. Electric Lighting Company had been founded back in 1878 by Edward Weston, developer of an arc lighting system, Moses Farmer, expert in electric generators, and Maxim, expert in incandescent lighting systems. The company sent Latimer to London in the fall of 1881 to establish an incandescent lamp department for the Maxim-Weston Electric Light Company there. But there was bias in Britain too. The men in that operation resented Latimer's leadership so much he returned to America in disappointment.

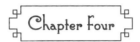

Chapter Four

Edison Wins the Patent Wars, with Latimer

Latimer's the Man I Want

Notwithstanding such experience and success, Latimer was sometimes left looking for work. This was the position he found himself in, after his return from Britain, despite his achievements, and despite how respected he was among the great men of invention of the late nineteenth century and early twentieth.

At a key point in Latimer's career, his friend Charles G. Perkins helped him get re-established. Latimer and Perkins were about the same age and they both started their careers in electric lighting at about the same time at the U.S. Electric Lighting Company, Hiram Maxim's company in Bridgeport, Connecticut, Thomas Edison's top competitor. Perkins had been in charge of installing the first commercial incandescent lighting system (excepting Edison's installation on a steamship), in the vaults of a New York safe deposit company.

Latimer had left for London in late 1881 to start an incandescent light factory there, for the Maxim-Weston Electric Lighting Company, as previously noted. But the British were no more willing than Americans to take direction from a black man, no matter how accomplished.

When Latimer returned to the U.S. a year later, he actually found it difficult to land steady employment. In his memoirs, Latimer recalls that when he returned from England in 1882, he "found the ranks closed up and every place filled."

In the five years following the end of Reconstruction in 1877, when Rutherford Hayes cut that deal with the Democrats and southerners to become President in exchange for the Republicans and northerners turning a blind eye to the violence and loss of civil rights in the south, racism had hardened in the country's culture. African Americans began to migrate north and west in the thousands. And in 1881, the year before Latimer returned to the U.S., Tennessee passed the first Jim Crow laws, segregating rail transportation.

It was Perkins that brought Latimer in as a close colleague at Imperial Electric Light Company, when Latimer couldn't find steady employment, and then at Mather Electric Light Company. But both companies were struggling against Thomas Edison's fast-expanding firm.

Like so many of Latimer's white peers, Perkins went on to great financial success; though Latimer did do very well economically when compared to African Americans of his period. The Perkins Electric Lamp Company was founded in 1889. But its lamp work came to a screeching halt when Edison, with the help of his top patent expert by this time, Lewis Latimer, settled a patent dispute with Perkins. No matter, as the Perkins Electric Switch Company was founded the next year, in 1890. There, Perkins developed electric switches that were broadly adopted. He later founded Arrow Electrical Wiring Devices that through mergers led to the power management giant of today, Eaton Corporation.

Latimer Makes Monopolies for Edison

It's 1884. This is the year Latimer is hired by Edison. Latimer starts out as a special assistant to Edison's general counsel Richard N. Dyer.

Latimer's new office is in 65 Fifth Avenue, the headquarters for the parent of Edison's expanding constellation of companies. Edison had moved his focus and family to New York three years earlier. One of Edison's so-called muckers (the men who had worked at his labs at Menlo Park in the

**Edison Electric Light Co. headquarters at 65 Fifth Avenue in Manhattan,
where Lewis Latimer started working in Edison's Engineering Department in 1884**

late eighteen-seventies and early eighteen-eighties), Francis Jehl, wrote this decades later about their first headquarters in Manhattan, in his "Menlo Park Reminiscences":

"The work done at '65' marked the beginning of the practical introduction of Edison's system, and what we know as the electrical industry. Sixty-five Fifth Avenue is a historical spot; it was the birthplace of a new epoch following that of Menlo Park; there, a new turning point in our modern civilization began."

It is also in 1884 that Thomas Edison's companies are increasingly prosecuting patent rights, aggressively, contesting a German patent, of the Swan incandescent lamp. Edison wins. He declares victory. Asserting his global primacy, the Wizard of Menlo Park says:

"The effect of the decision is in the highest degree important, not only there but here and in every other country, for it practically affirms that every other incandescent lamp is an infringement upon the Edison patent."

To understand Edison, to understand Latimer and his relationship with Edison and role in Edison's success and fame, one must fully appreciate how invention and patent litigation to secure the economic fruits of invention proceeded in the late nineteenth century. This is not a new point of view. For instance, Graham Moore's "The Last Days of Night," the acclaimed 2016 historical novel about the circuit wars of Edison, Nikola Tesla and George Westinghouse revolves around someone else, a name nearly lost to history, Paul Cravath. But it was Cravath, a twenties-something patent attorney, who ultimately structured the works of the three founding fathers of the electricity industry, going back and forth between them. Though Cravath is little remembered by the public at large, the three giants of electricity surely recognized his importance and essential role.

Edison saw his success as mastering patents strategically. It then comes as little surprise that he prized Latimer, who had led the patent work for his top competitors and patented himself key pieces of the lighting puzzle, the filament (often referred to then as the carbon), filament production and the filament's electrical connection.

Edison told his managers at the British Edison Electric Company this in 1882:

"Do not fail to remember the fact that there are 8 or 9 things in our system of general distribution [of electricity], any one of which if maintained will give us the commercial monopoly of the general distribution business and the patents which we are now coming out and which will come out in the course of the next year will be just as important in maintaining the monopoly as the patents which have already been issued."

Invention, a Blood Sport

Travel back to the late nineteenth century, to the world in which the great names of invention walked. Communication is by post and telegraph. Transportation is by horse, carriage and rail. Energy is by brute strength of animals and man, and steam engines.

The inventors cannot work in the night or inside their shops in the day except by the inconstant light from flame. They cannot know of scientific advances across continents or across their city except by newspaper, books, conversation and correspondence.

Invention is frantic and personal. It is incremental and contested. Rather, it is more than that. It is a blood sport. Fame and fortune are fiercely fought for and won for posterity, in tests of will and determination. As Hiram Maxim often commented, when complaining about Thomas Edison besting him, cunning in securing financial patronage, and talented craftsman and lawyers, was seemingly more important in the fight than scientific ingenuity.

From a 2012 Michigan Law Review article entitled "The Myth of the Sole Inventor:"

"The canonical story of the lone genius inventor is largely a myth. Edison didn't invent the lightbulb; he found a bamboo fiber that worked better as a filament in the lightbulb developed by Sawyer and Man, who in turn built on lighting work done by others. Bell filed for his telephone patent on the very same day as an independent inventor, Elisha Gray; the case ultimately went to the U.S. Supreme Court, which filled an entire volume of the United States Reports resolving the question of whether Bell could have a patent despite the fact that he hadn't actually gotten the invention to work at the time he filed …

Bell's iconic status owes as much to his victories in court and in the marketplace as to his work at the lab bench …

Edison found commercial success with his bamboo filament, which lasted longer than other carbonized vegetable materials. But bamboo didn't turn out to be the future; subsequent inventors came up with still better filaments in short order ..."

Lewis Latimer was in the forefront in perfecting the electric light bulb's filament. His inexpensive method for producing longer-lasting filaments, earned him his third patent on January 17, 1882, "Process of Manufacturing Carbons." The U.S. Patent and Trademark Office did take an unusually long while to award the patent, eleven months, which might reflect Latimer's lack of resources and legal champions to push things along in the federal government.

But this was an important step in the development of electric lighting. The competing inventors all realized, including Edison, that millions of filaments and bulbs would need to be manufactured economically. Alas, though Latimer likely did all the work, the patent as we have noted was assigned to the U.S. Electric Lighting Company.

Latimer then took a second step in early 1881, on April 18, two months after submitting "Process for Manufacturing Carbons." The application, "Electric Lamp," described a better method for connecting the filament to the lead wires in the base of a lamp, which earned him his second patent on September 13, 1881, just five months after the submission, a patent that he shared with Joseph V. Nichols. Both of them worked at the U.S. Electric Lighting Company and Nichols had earned a patent on his own eight months earlier that focused on perfecting the light bulb's glass globe.

The Latimer and Nichols patent reads:

"In order to secure a more perfect electrical contact between the carbons [filaments] and the wires, the ends of the former may be previously coated with copper or platinum. With this form of clamp all nuts, screws, or pins and similar accessories are dispensed with.

The conductors make contact with the carbons at considerable distance from the incandescent portion, so that the permanency of the connections is insured, and as the wires are by this means protected in great measure from the heat developed, they may be of copper, whereby the cost of the lamps is greatly reduced.

The wires are flattened for a short distance from their ends for securing greater contact-surface and flexibility ..."

Latimer took a third step that summer, on September 7, 1881, with his application for a patent entitled "Globe Supporter for Electric Lamps."

Six months later, he and John Tregoning received the patent, Latimer's fourth. Though, once again, the patent was assigned to the U.S. Electric Lighting Company.

Tregoning is better remembered as one of the founding fathers of management science, inventory controls, and cost accounting. His landmark book, "A Treatise on Factory Management," published in 1891, paved the way for the early twentieth century giants on management: Frederick A. Halsey, who you can blame for the U.S. not adopting the metric system, Henry Gantt, as in the ubiquitous Gantt chart, and Frederick Winslow Taylor, who pioneered the scientific study of work processes.

Latimer also witnessed Hiram Maxim's patent for an electric lamp, on March 9, 1880, about one month after Edison filed for his electric lighting patent. And, he witnessed Maxim's patent for producing filaments two weeks later, on March 22. Undoubtedly, Latimer played an essential role in these two inventions though he was relegated to a witness on both patents, by Maxim.

Latimer later made a name for himself in Edison's employ in the patent infringement suit, Edison Electric Light Company versus U.S. Electric Lighting Company. In other words, Latimer's new company was suing his old company. Edison alleged that lamp patents of inventor William Sawyer and Albon Man (who funded Sawyer's work), which had been assigned to Latimer's old company, infringed on Edison's patent for lamp filaments. Arguably no one knew more about the truth of the matter than Latimer.

Edison and Latimer

It is impossible for us to know much about the relationship between Thomas Edison and Lewis Latimer. After all, Edison had many of the brightest minds of the world working for him in the eighteen-eighties and Latimer was but one of them. Despite what most of us have heard about Edison, he wanted his experimentation to be pointed and purposeful – not random and repetitive – to discover the underlying scientific truths. And he wanted the best thinkers who relentlessly researched all the experimentation worldwide to work on his experimentation. Latimer fit the bill though he was self-taught while surrounded by colleagues who were brought up in wealthy families and attended the best schools where they received advanced degrees in science and engineering.

However, there is one conversation between Edison and Latimer that is documented for posterity. Edison had founded his Edison Phonograph

Company on October 8, 1887. He then introduced the so-called Improved Phonograph in May of 1888 and the co-called Perfected Phonograph soon after.

At this time, on June 16, 1888, Latimer jotted down this brief handwritten note to Edison on Edison Electric Light Company stationary:

"Dear Sir,

As the fourth of July is near at hand, I venture to hope that you may deem the enclosed lines, a fit and proper speech for the Phonograph, to make on the celebration of that day.

Trusting that you will not be wasting valuable time in reading them,

I am very Respectfully,

Your L.N. Latimer"

Some historians have read into these words that their formality suggests that the relationship between Edison and Latimer, who had joined Edison's men three years earlier, was slight. This supposition seems like quite a leap. Aside from the fact that Latimer was by nature mild-mannered and even deferential to his many famous bosses, in the culture of the eighteen-eighties it was likely common to employ such word constructions particularly among Edison's men when relating to the Wizard of Menlo Park.

One can see that Edison has annotated Latimer's note as follows:

"Thank him and say I will put it on and send cylinder to England.

T. Edison"

Edison's phonographs at that point recorded sound on cylinders and permanent recordings were manufactured in England.

Four days later, on June 20, 1888, there's a brief typed reply to Latimer, on plain note paper, signed by Edison's private secretary on that date, Alfred O. Tate:

"Dear Sir:

Mr. Edison asks me to thank you for the verses on the Phonograph enclosed with your letter under date16th inst. Mr. Edison is going to put these verses on a cylinder and send them to England.

A.O.T, Private Secretary"

Edison General Electric Co.'s new headquarters at 42 Broad Street in Manhattan, where Lewis Latimer worked in the Law Department starting in 1890

Latimer joined the company's Legal Department in 1890, the same year that Edison General Electric built its new headquarters and moved to 42 Broad Street. A contemporary biographical sketch stated:

> "… he made drawings for Court exhibits, had charge of the library, inspected infringing plants in various parts of the country, and testified as to facts in a number of cases, without materially encouraging the opposing counsel. He also did considerable searching for which his previous experience, and a moderate knowledge of French and German qualified him, rendering efficient service along these lines in the historical filament case and others of this period, involving basic patents."

There is an old grainy monochrome photo of the Legal Department, with four men and two women posing in the serious style of that period's photos. The six of them are buttoned-down, the two women particularly, and frowning almost. What is unusual for photos of that time, quite unusual in fact, is that one of the pictured professionals is a black man. In this photo, though, Latimer appears to fit perfectly within this group.

Latimer Discredits Goebel Defense

Around the time of the photo, Latimer continued to play a key role in the aggressive prosecution of Edison's patent rights, and he began to play this role in the landmark Oconto Incandescent Lamp Case. In the process, he obliterated the so-called Goebel defense in patent law.

The Edison Electric Light Company had sued three manufacturers of incandescent lamps in 1892, to obtain preliminary injunctions to close down their production of incandescent light bulbs, claiming the three companies were infringing on an Edison patent. How did these companies defend themselves? They said the Edison patent was void because it was not a novelty. Heinrich Goebel had invented the light bulb, they said, before Edison had, though Goebel never secured a patent. And, though Goebel had supposedly used only for himself this incandescent bulb that he crafted more than two decades before the Edison patent.

Hence, the Goebel defense, that had the potential to defang many a patent infringement lawsuit. The defendant would merely need to show that someone – anyone – had been tinkering in their shop on a similar idea on or before the patent-holding inventor's work, even though the tinkerer had never made this known to the U.S. Patent and Trademark Office or to anyone actually. With such a showing, the patent-holding inventor had no right to restrict defendants from the economic use of the idea.

By 1893, when the case proceeded, Goebel was already seventy-five. He would pass away later that same year. Though he and his tinkering were critical to the case, Goebel didn't care that much about how the case was decided. It was those three companies that cared, defending their light bulb manufacturing businesses, as well as Edison's men who aspired to defeat and disable these operations and indeed any and all their competition.

Latimer filed an affidavit and a memo, "Mr. Latimer's Theory on the Goebel Lamp Case." After extensive investigation, he showed decisively that the Goebel lamps weren't originals predating the Edison patent. Rather, they were reproductions of later works by Charles Perkins and glass blower Gustav E. Muller, who Latimer had quite conveniently worked with at U.S. Electric Lighting, Hiram Maxim's company in the early eighteen-eighties.

Edison's Law Department including Lewis Latimer, standing second from the right

Latimer constantly saw connections between science, engineering and art. His lifelong love for these conceptual overlaps is evident in the minutes of the Association of Edison Illuminating Companies annual meeting in 1893. Thomas Edison and his closest colleagues had founded this elite organization eight years prior.

According to Jehl's "Menlo Park Reminiscences":

"He [Edison] was delighted to attend the conventions of the Association of Edison Illuminating Companies; he enjoyed occasions where the presence of his great personality gave luster and publicity."

AEIC remains quite active today, celebrating its hundred and thirty-five year anniversary in 2020.

Industry giant John Irvin Beggs, who had served as AEIC's president since its inception, read out loud to the meeting a poem penned by Latimer. These verses of biting sarcasm were cleverly entitled:

Lines to Heinrich Goebel
"Inventor of the Incandescent Lamp" (?)

With brilliant humor, Latimer mocked the Goebel defense. Goebel's so-called invention of the light bulb is depicted in the poem as an unobserved act that is much later seized upon by opportunistic lawyers as the foundation for their arguments. Here's Latimer's twenty lines, as read to the 1893 meeting by AEIC's president:

Gods! That a man like this should live
Beneath Columbia's sky,
All these long years in secrecy,

Hid from each prying eye;
Unknown, unsung, unpraised of men,
While warring factions rage –
Forgetful that his mind conceived

The wonder of the age.
Nor he alone; but all who'd seen
The triumph of his skill,
Equally they forgetful were

And would remain so still,
Had not some legal leader's eye
Espied them from afar,
And, with the magic of his will,

Brought them to Justice's bar.
Oh, memory! thy ways profound
In voiceless awe we see,
And, wandering 'mid a maze of doubt,

Mistake a lie for thee.

Before the reading, Beggs addressed this august meeting of electricity industry leaders. Beggs says with equal humor, "… with the permission of the Chair and the Association, I will read it to you and suggest that it be embalmed in the Minutes."

After the reading, which must have been quite an entertainment for all, all white men undoubtedly, Beggs added:

"I understand that one of the attorneys stated that he would have presented this in lieu of his argument had he known of it, and he says it would have covered the whole case. It is apparently a sort of reverie by Mr. Latimer, one of Mr. [William J.] Jenks' assistants, who is one of the old-timers in the lamp industry, and who has been engaged in the lamp litigation."

John Beggs would have commanded the respect of those present. He dominated the electric industry in Wisconsin, as a director or officer of most of the industry players simultaneously. He built the historic Public Service Building in Milwaukee which still stands today and is the headquarters for We Energies.

There is much that one can say about Beggs' career, from electrifying a house of worship for the first time, to developing many of our modern methods in depreciation accounting, to dying as the richest Wisconsinite. But, Beggs was also at the table of that famous banquet along with the top officers of the nation's largest power companies, at AEIC's 1896 annual meeting.

Why is this gathering famous? Because it was there that a young engineer from Detroit was introduced to Thomas Edison. The engineer, Henry Ford, then outlined his grandiose plan for a gasoline-fueled automobile industry. Edison then "brought his fist down on the table with a bang and said, 'Young man, that's the thing; you have it. Keep at it.'" And, as the old saying goes, the rest is history.

As the Goebel case was getting underway, in 1892, Thomas Edison was losing control of his company. The very powerful financier J.P. Morgan, concerned that Edison wasn't acknowledging the primacy of alternating current systems over direct current systems, and was falling behind competitively, merged the Thomson-Houston Company with Edison General Electric Company.

It soon became clear that the Thomson-Houston people were in the driver's seat, relative to those from Edison General Electric. Thomson-Houston's Charles Coffin became the chief executive officer of the merged company, which promptly dropped Edison from its name. The company has been known thereafter as General Electric.

Coffin's successor as General Electric's chief executive was Owen Young. It was Young who founded Public Utilities Reports in 1914, the firm which a few years later started publishing my magazine, Public Utilities Fortnightly.

Before reading aloud Latimer's poem at AEIC's 1893 annual meeting, John Beggs mentioned that it had been Luther Stieringer that brought the poem to his attention. We don't know how Stieringer had come by Latimer's poem. But it must be said that Stieringer is apparently one more giant of the electric industry's development that Latimer had some substantial dealings with.

Stieringer was the go-to guy for Edison and just about everybody as to how incandescent electric lighting should be used (as opposed to gas lighting), to provide uniform illumination, or for decorative purposes, inside and outside, with colored lights as well, or even for large expositions. He was the one who designed the lighting for the World's Columbian Exposition, an enormous fair that took place in Chicago in 1893 and that was visited by an estimated one-third of all Americans.

But What Do I Do Now?

The decisive battle of the war of currents between Thomas Edison and George Westinghouse, with Nikola Tesla much more than an ordinary warrior in the conflict, was fought at the World's Columbian Exposition in 1893.

To celebrate the four hundredth anniversary of Christopher Columbus' landing in the Americas, the spectacular hundred and eighty-four day fair – which brought a third of the nation's populace to Chicago to see the future and featured everything from the first Ferris wheel to the first serial killer – has been ofttimes depicted in popular culture. There's Erik Larson's 2003 book, "The Devil in the White City: Murder, Magic, and Madness at the Fair That Changed America," for example, and the star-studded 2017 movie, "The Current War."

It has been little-noticed that the movie featured the British actor Simon Manyonda of South African and Zimbabwean descent playing the role of Lewis Latimer. Latimer is shown realistically in the film as a clever and studious man in Thomas Edison's employ – and the sole one of color – advising Edison as the Wizard of Menlo Park endeavors to beat down all of those with a competing claim to electricity's development. Hiram Maxim, Latimer's former employer, was one. George Westinghouse was another.

The movie captures the character of Latimer, Edison and the other warriors of current. One scene early on opens with Edison throwing a tantrum in front of twenty of his men gathered in the laboratory, after discovering George Westinghouse had taken an advantage in the war, using Hiram Maxim's light bulbs:

Thomas Edison, played by actor Benedict Cumberbatch: No! How did he get the bulbs? {Edison pauses, about to explode in anger.} What a roaring silence from the brightest minds of America.

Lewis Latimer, played by actor Simon Manyonda: He's using Hiram's design.

Edison: {Now, in a rage.} Which Hiram stole from me! Sue him!

Latimer: We already did. The Court upheld his patent.

Edison: I'm talking about Westinghouse. Find an angle.

Samuel Insull, played by actor Tom Holland: Take a trip to Barrington and see for yourself {at George Westinghouse's laboratory}.

Edison: {He's really shouting now.} You're not even slightly irked that fifteen years of work have been filched from right under your eyes. Not again! I built a system here and you go shopping for patents to cobble together something to legally steal what is mine. If bulbs are a battle, then nail him on the dynamos {that is, the power generator patents}.

Insull: We can't. He's not even using direct current, sir.

Edison: He's using alternating?

Later in the film, Edison slumps down, disconsolately, on porch steps looking onto the laboratory grounds:

Insull: Can I get you anything, sir?

Edison: A time machine. {The script writer took a liberty here. H.G. Wells' science fiction novella "The Time Machine" wasn't yet published, not until 1895, when it popularized the idea of time travel.}

Insull: Yes, well, if I ever find one, I'll travel back to this moment and give it to you. Did you read the proposal?

Edison: I'm not diverting what I've got left of my resources and lighting up a fair.

Insull: It's much more than a fair, sir. A third of the country will get on trains to Chicago to try and see this city of light. Every window, every street lamp, a sign that says that the race is over, and we won. Why spend your final dollars traveling this country to show everyone your electricity when they're all traveling to the same place to try and see it anyway?

Edison: Because in a year they'll rip it down.

Insull: Only after thirty million people have seen it, yes. {A long pause.} Westinghouse is placing a bid. {Which further demoralizes Edison.}

Edison: {Latimer walking by, nattily-attired, with a top hat in hand.} Nice hat. Looks expensive.

Latimer: I owned this before I worked for you, Mr. Edison.

Edison: I think you are working for me. He's {Westinghouse is} using my bulbs.

Latimer: His patents are in order. Do you want my advice? You keep saying Westinghouse's current will kill people. So, in lieu of evidence, why don't you provide it?

It's highly doubtful Latimer planted the notion in Edison's head, to demonstrate that Westinghouse's alternating current was more dangerous than direct current, by electrocuting dogs, a horse and an elephant. Ultimately, through the schemes of an Edison man Harold Brown, New York was persuaded to electrocute William Kemmler, who murdered his mistress with an axe, carrying out the death sentence with thirteen hundred and then two thousand volts, of alternating current naturally, to discredit AC. Though note that Brown schemed in the late eighteen-eighties to have Kemmler electrocuted, which took place on August 6, 1890, a couple of years before Edison, Insull and even Latimer might have discussed the great fair that planned to open in Chicago on May 1, 1893.

Chicago's Columbian Exposition Changes Everything

There is no record of Latimer visiting the Columbian Exposition in Chicago, though it seems quite likely he did. During the six months it was open, the first of May through the thirtieth of October, the fair's visitors numbered twenty-seven million and three hundred thousand. That's actually forty-three percent of the population counted in the 1890 Census, sixty-three million. On Chicago Day, the ninth of October, attendance peaked at a remarkable seven hundred and fifty-one thousand. Given Latimer's experience and intellectual curiosity, and his financial means, he must have gone, if not for his employer at the time – General Electric Company (founded April 15, 1892 through the merger of Edison General Electric and Thomson-Houston Electric) – then for himself.

Latimer probably signed the "Petition to Congress to Repeal the Act Closing the World's Columbian Exposition on Sundays," as did most of Thomas Edison's employees. Edison had publicly and strongly supported the initiative to overcome the so-called blue laws. The fair managers waffled, at first closing on Sundays, then reversing course and opening on Sundays, and finally reverting to closing on Sundays.

And, whether Latimer went to Chicago or not, he was certainly aware about the controversy about the Columbian Exposition overlooking African Americans' contributions to the progress of civilization. Ida B. Wells, born into slavery in Mississippi during the Civil War, shined a light on how the fair sidestepped the role of blacks in America and tirelessly worked to convince the organizers to effect changes. With her co-author Frederick Douglass, she wrote and then widely distributed her pamphlet, "The Reason Why the Colored American is Not in the World's Columbian Exhibition." The pamphlet included this eloquent pleading:

> "Those visitors to the World's Columbian Exposition … especially foreigners will naturally ask … Why are not the colored people who constitute so large an element of the American population, and who have contributed so large a share to American greatness, more visibly present and better represented in this World's Exposition? Why are they not taking part in this glorious celebration of the four-hundredth anniversary of the discovery of their country? Are they so dull and stupid as to feel no interest in this great event?"

The seven and a half million African Americans were nearly twelve percent of all Americans in the 1890 Census. Remarkably, twenty-five years after emancipation, ninety percent of the country's black population remained living in the south. (In comparison, in the last Census, of 2010, after the Great Migration of the twentieth century, fifty-six and a half percent of the country's black population lived in the south.) In 1890, they were actually the solid majority in South Carolina and Mississippi, and were half of all Louisianans.

The demographics in the states of the northeast, midwest and west were very different. For example, African Americans were just one and a half percent of the population in the Columbian Exposition's state, Illinois. And, they were just over one percent of the population in Latimer's home state, New York, with only seventy-two thousand black residents in 1890.

Naturally, the experiences of northern blacks who lived free as a very small minority in an urban society contrasted with the experiences of southern blacks who had lived in bondage as a very large minority – in many counties, as a majority of the total population – in a rural society, and who were freed by emancipation. Most northern blacks were literate and many were well-educated. This was not the case of course for southern blacks, whose opportunities for education and advancement only opened up after 1865.

The 1870 Census found that eighty percent of African Americans, age fourteen and over, were illiterate, while the illiteracy rate for whites was eleven and a half percent. By 1890, twenty years later, despite some progress during the Reconstruction years of 1865 through 1876, mainly, the illiteracy rate remained high among southern blacks. It was seventy-two percent for blacks in Louisiana, age ten and over, sixty-nine percent in Alabama, sixty-seven percent in Georgia, sixty-four percent in South Carolina, sixty-one percent in Mississippi, and sixty percent in North Carolina.

But the illiteracy rate for blacks in Massachusetts, where Lewis Latimer was born, and where he had worked with Alexander Graham Bell, was fourteen percent in 1890. And, it was fifteen percent in Connecticut, where Latimer had worked with Hiram Maxim, initially. And, it was seventeen percent in New York, where Latimer lived most of his adult life, and where he worked with Thomas Edison.

Everything we know of Lewis Latimer tells us he would fervently agree with this statement in the pamphlet by Wells and Douglass. Indeed, Latimer likely was among the most passionate about the fair's representation – and obvious omissions – of African Americans' contributions to the progress of technology and civilization in the U.S.

Wells working with other black women succeeded to a degree. Two African Americans were added as staff at the fair's Board of Control. Black women formed the Women's Columbian Auxiliary Association and were permitted to feature lecturers at the World's Congress of Representative Women.

There was Anna Julia Haywood Cooper. Born into slavery in North Carolina, and ten years younger than Latimer, Cooper received her master's degree in mathematics at Oberlin College five years before the fair in Chicago, and authored one year before the fair, "A Voice from the South: By a Black Woman of the South," which discussed black feminism. Later in life, in 1924, she became the fourth African American women to receive a doctorate.

And there was Hallie Quinn Brown, principal of the Tuskegee Institute. Born free in Pennsylvania, a child of freed slaves, and a year younger than Latimer. Brown was a beloved speaker and public reader before large audiences and she spoke at the Republican National Convention in 1924. She led President Calvin Coolidge's campaign efforts aimed at African American women at a time when almost all blacks were loyal to the Republican Party.

And there was Fannie Jackson Coppin, born into slavery in Washington D.C., and eleven years older than Latimer. In her twelfth year, her aunt purchased Coppin's freedom. She was the first black teacher at the Oberlin Academy, on the campus of Oberlin College, and the first black school principal, at Philadelphia's Institute for Colored Youth, now the historically black university, Cheyney University. Her speech at the fair in Chicago was entitled, "The intellectual progress of the colored women of the United States since the Emancipation Proclamation."

And there was Sarah Jane Woodson Early of Tennessee, born free in Ohio, and much older than Latimer, by twenty-three years. Woodson Early was a leader in the Women's Christian Temperance Union, which was a major political force in that period, and her speech at the fair in Chicago was entitled, "The Organized Efforts of the Colored Women of the South to Improve Their Condition."

And, finally, there was Frannie Barrier Williams, vice president of the Illinois Women's Alliance and the fair's so-called Clerk in charge of Colored Interests in the Department of Publicity and Promotions. Williams later was a co-founder of the NAACP and then the sole black with a part in the eulogies of Susan B. Anthony at the National American Woman Suffrage Association convention in 1907.

Patent Control

Thomas Edison's companies and George Westinghouse's companies had been arch-rivals in the electrification of the country for a decade. After numerous suits and countersuits between the two warring camps, they finally found a way to cooperate, hoping to monopolize and divide the spoils. In 1896, they set up a Board of Patent Control. This brought a welcome truce to the constant warfare in the courts over patent rights.

William Johnson Jenks, who had headed the Legal Department of the Edison Electric Light Company in the late eighteen-eighties, and the successor entity, General Electric Company, in the early eighteen-nineties, was naturally selected to head the innocuous sounding Board of Patent Control.

Lewis Latimer as an elder statesman of electricity's development

And, of course, his longtime colleague, Lewis Latimer, now forty-eight, was selected to become the Board's chief draftsman and expert witness.

From 1883 to 1885, the period when Latimer found his way into the employment of Thomas Edison, Jenks was a manager at the Edison Electric Illuminating Company of Brockton, which pioneered Edison's three-wire underground system. His boss there was coincidentally William Lloyd Garrison, Jr., son of the great abolitionist who had played a leading role in defending Latimer's father from recapture by his father's former slave owner back in 1842.

Jenks was much more than the top legal officer for Edison's companies, where he supervised Latimer's work. A respected confidant of Edison, and a colleague of Latimer, Jenks authored for example a paper read before the American Institute of Electrical Engineers in December 1888, "Central Station Lighting, Six Years' Practical Experience with the Edison Chemical Meter," on measuring electric current. He had led Edison's projects over the preceding three years to light city streets with incandescents and central station power plants.

Chapter Five

Only One African American Among the Edison Pioneers

Black Royalty

The Flushing home of Lewis Latimer and his wife Mary Wilson Latimer, and daughters Jeanette and Louise, was a regular gathering place for black intellectuals and leaders of the early twentieth century. Aside from W.E.B. Du Bois and Paul Robeson, previously mentioned, visitors to this salon for discourse on Holly Avenue included author Jessie Redmon Fauset, who later spurred many Harlem Renaissance authors in the nineteen-twenties. And, composer Harry T. Burleigh, who later worked with the great Antonin Dvorak.

And, author and composer James Weldon Johnson, who President Theodore Roosevelt appointed as U.S. Consul to Venezuela and Nicaragua, and who later was the first African-American professor at New York University. In 1900, to help celebrate Abraham Lincoln's birthday, he wrote the poem "Lift Every Voice and Sing" that was set to music five years later by his younger brother John Rosamond Johnson and came to be known as the negro national anthem after the National Association for the Advancement of Colored People, the NAACP, dubbed it so in 1919.

John Rosamond Johnson was of course another regular at the Latimer home in Queens. J. Rosamond trained at the New England Conservatory, studied in London and then went on to a successful show business career with another brother, Bob Cole. Together, J. Rosamond and Cole wrote the first black musicals – notably without the typical racist stereotypes of that period – and ultimately broke through the barriers and wrote musicals for predominantly white audiences.

First performed in 1905, when Lewis Latimer was fifty-seven, Lift Every Voice and Sing must have become a favorite at his Flushing home. Here's an excerpt from the lyrics:

We have come over a way that with
tears has been watered,

We have come, treading our path
through the blood of the slaughtered,

Out from the gloomy past,

'Til now we stand at last

Where the white gleam of our bright
star is cast.

Another guest at the Latimer home was civic leader Eugene Kinkell Jones of the National Urban League. Jones was thirty-seven years younger than Lewis Latimer. The passion of Jones was to break down the barriers to black employment in the nineteen-twenties and nineteen-thirties particularly. He joined the Franklin Roosevelt Administration in 1933 as an advisor on Negro Affairs at the U.S. Department of Commerce and became a member of FDR's so-called Black Cabinet, which at the time was a breakthrough. It wasn't until 1966, decades later, that an African American actually joined a President's Cabinet, when President Lyndon Johnson appointed Robert Weaver to be Secretary of Housing and Urban Development.

Latimer was iconic among the leaders of the black community. Back in 1897, his friend Theodore Greener connected Latimer with Booker T. Washington, the president of Tuskegee Institute. That same year, Washington invited George Washington Carver to head Tuskegee's agricultural department.

Later, Washington asked Latimer to develop and draw a plan of the campus buildings and grounds at Tuskegee.

Carver's greatest accomplishment while as a professor there was to urge and popularize systematic crop rotation, which had an enormous impact on southern farm productivity, which had deteriorated from repeated plantings of cotton, and an enormous impact as well on the nutrition of southerners. While Carver tirelessly promoted the uses of peanuts (and sweet potatoes too), alas, he didn't invent nor claim to invent everyone's favorite, peanut butter.

Booker T.

Washington, born into slavery in southwest Virginia in 1856, was arguably the most prominent African American leader in the years before and after the turn of the century. He is perhaps best remembered for his Atlanta Compromise speech in 1895, urging black progress through education and entrepreneurship. The speech sparked a north-south division between Washington and W.E.B. Du Bois, who lived in the north, and who called the southerner Washington "the great accommodator." Du Bois advocated greater political activism.

And, Washington is also well-remembered as the first African American to dine at the White House, a dinner that erupted into a national controversy. Theodore Roosevelt had just become president of the United States after the assassination of William McKinley in Buffalo, New York on September 6, 1901. McKinley died from the gunshot wounds and gangrene eight days later, on September 14.

On October 16, at eight that evening, Washington was admitted to the private apartment of the White House for dinner. Roosevelt, after having just moved into the White House, had invited Washington to dine with him, his family and his hunting buddy and Colorado politician, Philip Stewart. When Roosevelt was Governor of New York, he frequently had black guests to dinner and sometimes asked them to stay overnight.

Roosevelt found that it was a big deal when, following the dinner, the south's indignation exploded on the very next day. Senator Benjamin (Pitchfork Ben) Tillman of South Carolina infamously said, my apologies to the reader ahead of time for having to recall these terrible words from the Senator:

"The action of President Roosevelt in entertaining that nigger will necessitate our killing a thousand niggers in the South before they learn their place again."

While the President did respond, "I shall have him to dine as often as I please," Roosevelt did so more discretely from then on, and never again for dinner in the evening (lunch being considered less of an afront to white supremacists like Tillman).

Notwithstanding the uproar, Roosevelt and Washington cut a deal at the dinner that placed a few blacks into key federal government positions. This was somewhat of a breakthrough. Washington carefully chose these individuals for the so-called Black Cabinet – predecessor to the far more influential Black Cabinet of President Franklin Roosevelt in the nineteen-thirties and nineteen-forties – which caused his rival in the civil rights community, Du Bois, to accuse Washington of maintaining an exclusive Tuskegee Machine.

Washington and Du Bois

In the rivalry, Lewis Latimer must have sided with Washington. The two men accepted segregation, reluctantly of course, but did so while emphasizing the educational and economic advancement of African Americans. Du Bois and his supporters instead believed it was vital to challenge segregation head on.

Du Bois was more idealistic, but he could easily point to the frustrations of the more pragmatic approach by the Washington camp. While President Theodore Roosevelt was personally comfortable with African Americans, the President allowed bigoted federal government employees to limit black employees' access to office cafeterias, bathrooms and lockers. More important, Roosevelt's response to riots in Atlanta and Brownsville, Texas, in late 1906, was disappointing to say the least by civil rights leaders of all suasions.

Du Bois, in disgust and desperation, turned to the Democrats and supported their candidate, William Jennings Bryant, in the election of 1908 against the eventual winner William Howard Taft of the Republican Party, the party that African Americans were historically loyal to. Yet, immediately upon taking office, Taft followed the line of the so-called Lily Whites in race relations.

Latimer and Civil Rights

What was Lewis Latimer doing during the election of 1908? Three years earlier he had founded with others the fully-integrated First Unitarian Church in his Flushing neighborhood of Queens, New York which the founders incorporated in 1908 with Latimer as a charter member.

Through most of President Taft's administration, until 1911, Latimer remained a key employee at the Board of Patent Control originally formed by Thomas Edison's men and George Westinghouse to corner the market on electric lighting systems. Finally the U.S. Justice Department caused the dissolution of the Board on the basis of violating the Sherman Antitrust Act of 1890.

Back in 1895, Lewis Latimer's friend Theodore Greener, the first African-American Harvard grad, urged Latimer to attend a meeting of the National Conference of Colored Men in Detroit. Latimer was unable to attend but wrote these eloquent words for the attendees advocating the common cause of white and black citizens as the Reverend Dr. Martin Luther King would in the mid-twentieth century:

"… it is necessary that we should show the people of this country that we who have by our martyrdom (suffering) under the lash; by our heroism on the battlefield; by our Christian forbearance (patience) beneath an overwhelming burden of injustice; and by our submission to the laws of the native land, proven ourselves worthy citizens of our common country …

If our cause be made the common cause, and all our claims and demands be founded on justice and humanity, recognizing that we must wrong no man in winning OUR rights, I have faith to believe that the Nation will respond to our plea for equality before the law, security under the law, and an opportunity, by and through maintenance of the law, to enjoy with our fellow citizens of all races and complexions the blessings guaranteed us under the Constitution, of 'life, liberty, and the pursuit of happiness.'"

In the next year, on May 18, 1896, the U.S. Supreme Court upholds the de jure racial segregation of so-called separate but equal facilities in the notorious Plessy versus Ferguson decision. In so doing, the Supreme Court endorsed the Jim Crow laws for the next seven decades.

In one poignant phrasing in one of the most far-reaching Supreme Court decisions in American history, Associate Justice Henry Billings Brown writing for the overwhelming majority (except the lone dissenter being Associate Justice John M. Harlan) said this:

"A statute which implies merely a legal distinction between the white and colored races has no tendency to destroy the legal equality of the two races, or reestablish a state of involuntary servitude … [An implied distinction] must always exist so long as white men are distinguished from the other race by color … [It's a fallacy to assume that] the enforced separation of the two races stamps the colored race with a badge of inferiority … If this be so, it is not by reason of anything found in the act, but solely because the colored race chooses to put that construction upon it."

It was a tumultuous time in the striving for equality across citizens of all races. On November 10, 1898, for instance, an army of two thousand heavily-armed Red Shirts essentially revolted and seized the government of North Carolina's largest city, Wilmington, which had heretofore thrived as an integrated community, a rarity in the south following the collapse of Reconstruction. After murdering hundreds of blacks and white "carpetbaggers," and terrifying thousands, the Red Shirts presented the leading black men of Wilmington with the coup's "White Declaration of Independence," which the African American community bowed to, of course.

White Royalty

If you were reading the New York Times on Lincoln's Birthday in 1918, you might have spotted an article about a luncheon that took place on the day before. A luncheon? How is a luncheon newsworthy?

Then you would understand, immediately. This was no ordinary luncheon. A new organization called the Edison Pioneers had met to celebrate Thomas Edison's seventy-first birthday. According to the Times:

"The organization was formed recently, not only as a tribute to Mr. Edison, but as a step towards bringing together the most active influences in the electrical world."

In attendance, the Times listed, was a who's who of American business and technology. They had started their careers as essential assistants to Thomas Edison and now they were generally captains of industry themselves.

The group's president was Francis Robbins Upton, Edison's oldest associate, joining him in 1878, whom Edison called his mathematician and occasionally by the nickname, Culture. Upton was literally the first to receive a doctorate from Princeton University. As the ultimate evidence of Edison's faith in his mathematician, Upton published the world's first exposition of the invention of electric lighting and of the central power stations and electric distribution system that Edison's men planned to electrify the world, "Edison's Electric Light," an article in Scribner's, published only a few weeks after the invention in February of 1880. Ten years later, in 1890, Upton patented the first fire alarm and detector.

And, in the list of thirty-seven attendees was John F. Ott. He was Edison's close friend, who became the superintendent of the laboratory's machine shop. Ott held as many as twenty-two patents, some of them jointly with Edison.

Latimer and William Hammer

Also there at the luncheon was William Joseph Hammer. He had been one of Edison's earliest and most esteemed associates, and soon became chief engineer of Edison Lamp Works, and later head of British Edison Company. That William Hammer so respected Latimer probably helped to break down some barriers in the way of the African American polymath.

William Hammer had a life of firsts. Hammer was the co-inventor of watch and clock luminous dials. He was as well the first to propose radium as a cancer cure, working cooperatively with Pierre and Marie Curie, the discoverers of radium and polonium, for which they were awarded Nobel Prizes in 1903 for physics and 1910 for chemistry.

Hammer was also the first to build an electric sign lighted by incandescent bulbs. Of course, it spelled Edison in lights. It was placed over the organ in London's Crystal Palace concert hall.

This was likely where Latimer met Hammer, beginning a meaningful bond for both men. Drexel, Morgan & Co. (the predecessor to the financial giant J.P. Morgan & Co.), funded participation of the Edison lighting system at the Crystal Palace Exhibition in the spring of 1882, to kick-start Edison's business in Britain. So, Hammer was sent to work the exhibit in

**Edison Pioneers meet for the first time, including Lewis Latimer,
in the very front, second from the right**

London. Latimer was in London too, having started his work there to kick-start Maxim's business in Britain. Latimer and Hammer were competitors and colleagues.

In the diary of Latimer's wife Mary, we find these words as to what happened next:

> "Gus [probably Latimer's assistant], Lew and I went to Crystal Palace, staid {sic} until I was thoroughly tired out."

Later in Mary's London diary entries, she reveals something of Latimer's work ethic:

> "Lew is making a fine drawing of an invention of his, of some improvement in elevators and will see if he can get a patent on it. I hope it will be a success, he deserves to be successful for he works and studies all the time."

William Hammer was a man of firsts as previously said. He later invented the flashing electric sign. And, he was the first to buy an airplane in the U.S. As if this wasn't enough, his central power station in London, to power three thousand lamps, actually preceded the Pearl Street Station in Manhattan. Although, unlike Pearl Street, Holborn Viaduct was a temporary demonstration of Edison's central power station.

He played an absolutely critical role in Edison's invention of the light bulb. He had discovered what was initially called "Hammer's Phantom Shadow," that blackened the bulb, but which was unsurprisingly renamed after the boss, as the "Edison Effect." Whatever the effect's name, and whoever received the credit for finding it, this discovery led to the important invention of the diode vacuum tube in 1904.

He was also known for putting together an extensive collection of bulbs documenting for historians the first decades of electric incandescent lighting. The collection actually won the Grand Prize at the enormous St. Louis World's Fair of 1904. If you look at Hammer's case two, the eighth bulb from the right on the top shelf is labeled Latimer. It's an example of Latimer's invention while working for Hiram Maxim in 1881.

Other bulbs in case two were created by Maxim, George Westinghouse, Werner von Siemens and Joseph Swan, among the leading inventors of the light bulb in competition with Thomas Edison and at virtually the same time. The Westinghouse lamps were the same model used to illuminate the World's

Columbian Exposition in 1893 in Chicago. In another of Hammer's bulb exhibit's, the label for Latimer's lamp reads:

"This lamp was invented by a colored man, Mr. L.H. Latimer, in New York 1882, and was presented to me by Mr. Latimer in 1884."

Latimer and Hammer's Brother Edwin

Latimer was close to William Hammer's brother too, Edwin W. Hammer, also an Edison Pioneer. Latimer's last years of work, beginning in 1911, when the Board of Patent Control was dissolved, were for the engineering firm headed by Edwin Hammer and Elmer H. Schwarz that the two established six years earlier. Latimer worked as an electrical engineer at Hammer and Schwarz from 1911 to 1924, when he retired.

It was that year, 1924, when his wife Mary Wilson Latimer passed away. Lewis and Mary Wilson Latimer were married for fifty-one years.

As accomplished as was William Hammer, his brother Edwin was certainly an overachiever too. In September of 1896, when William J. Morton published his landmark book, "The X-Ray: Or, Photography of the Invisible and Its Value in Surgery," only nine months after Wilhelm Rontgen discovered the x-ray, his co-author was Edwin Hammer, who complemented Morton's medical expertise with his in electrical engineering. Morton and Edwin Hammer had taken the first x-rays of many body parts. Their book became a must-have for doctors, surgeons and dentists world-wide.

Other Edison Pioneers

Elmer Schwarz was another mover and shaker. He held several patents on electrical inventions. And, notably, he was a director of the Henry Street Settlement, a Lower East Side of Manhattan service to the poor founded in 1893 by Lillian Wald, where Latimer coincidentally (or not) taught mechanical drawing and English to recent immigrants, mostly Eastern European Jews. Once again, we can see how extraordinarily well-networked Latimer was.

Wald was also a civil rights activist. Though she was born into a wealthy German-Jewish family, Wald was a founding member of the National Association for the Advancement of Colored People, the NAACP.

John White Howell and his brother Wilson Stout Howell were there at the Edison Pioneers luncheon as well. A young Wilson was the first to lay electric wires underground for Edison. A young John, still enrolled at the Stevens Institute of Technology, calculated the required wire sizes for electric loads – lamps – for Edison.

John Howell invented a volt meter for the central power station. He made a deal with Edison and his secretary Samuel Insull, paying a royalty of three dollars per meter, which ultimately enriched John. He also worked closely with Lewis Latimer in Edison's constant litigation of patents, and authored the third section of Latimer's book, "Incandescent Electric Lighting," published in 1890 by the major scientific publishing house, D. Van Nostrand Company. This twenty-eight page section, entitled "The Maximum Efficiency of Incandescent Lamps," is highly quantitative befitting Howell's engineering training.

Latimer's Book

In contrast, the second section by Cornelius James Field, a product of Stevens' Institute of Technology like so many of Thomas Edison's men, entitled "Design and Operation of Incandescent Stations," in twenty-five pages, is an operations and cost analysis of central power stations like the one Edison erected at Pearl Street in Manhattan. And a tour, specifically of the power station that Edison Electric Illuminating had recently completed in Brooklyn, New York, in the fall of 1889, for which:

> "… the company [was] trying to secure the benefit of past experience in the larger stations of this class, both in the arrangement and kind of apparatus used, trying to secure at as economical a cost as possible the best plant for the purpose… We have, therefore, here, in a building 75 x 100 feet, apparatus and all departments complete for the generation and supply of current and power for a capacity of 40,000 lights, or the equivalent in light and power, and so arranged as to secure, as far as can be foreseen, continuous working of the plant and entire reliability in the furnishing of its current."

Field, at the time he authored this section of Latimer's book, was general manager and chief engineer of the Edison Electric Illuminating Company based in Brooklyn. But he would soon move on, and founded his own company. Later he became prominent in the growing field of electric railway plants, and he regularly lectured at the prestigious engineering societies and at Stevens' and Cornell University.

The first section by Lewis Latimer, seventy-six pages and beautifully-illustrated, entitled "Incandescent Electric Lighting," reflects Latimer's inclination to describe technological development with all the precision and clarity of a patent application to the government. Of particular interest is his common-sense explanation of how electricity is distributed from central power stations, the practice developed by Edison's men and used universally ever since:

> "When large districts of a city are lighted from a central station, what is termed the three-wire system, is generally employed, as it has economical advantages, which are not possessed by any other method that has been in practical operation up to the present time for commercial lighting on a large scale.
>
> In the two-wire system, the lamps are arranged between the two large conductors, in what are called multiple arc or parallel; that is they are arranged like the rounds of a ladder between the main conductors.
>
> This arrangement leaves each lamp independent of all others, so that any one may be turned off without interfering with those that remain burning. In order, however, that the lamps farthest removed from the generator shall have as much current as those nearest to it, the main conductor must of necessity be so large as to present practically no resistance to the passage of the current … It was to obviate this defect, that the three-wire system was invented by Mr. Thomas A. Edison.
>
> In practical electric lighting, the number of lamps receiving their current from a common central station, often runs up into thousands; and, as it is neither practicable nor desirable, to run these lamps all from one generator, a number of generators have to be combined together to furnish the necessary current, each generator having a capacity of a given number of lamps. These being the conditions under which lighting must be done, we will endeavor to make clear by comparison the advantages secured by the employment of the three-wire system."

In another passage, Latimer's poetic side comes out:

> "Like the light of the sun, it [electric lighting] beautifies all things on which it shines, and is no less welcome in the palace than in the humblest home."

Latimer's book was apparently successful and likely read across many nations as they developed their electric systems. After the first edition was published, in 1881, authored by William Edward Sawyer, it was revised for the revolutionary developments in this field during the eighteen-eighties (including the distribution of electricity from central power stations) and republished by the D. Van Nostrand Company, as Latimer writes:

"... the publishers have decided to re-issue this number of their Science Series, with the matter contained therein, thoroughly revised and brought down to date; and trust that the same generous appreciation which attended their first effort, will justify them in this attempt to give to the public a popular exposition of the art of electric lighting by incandescence."

The influential senior scientist on Edison's team, Arthur Kennelly, was critical of Latimer's original manuscript and may have prevailed upon Latimer to make significant edits. Kennelly was oddly Edison's key man in the late eighteen-eighties – together with Harold Brown – to persuade the public that alternating current was so dangerous it was suitable to carry out the death penalty. And then just a few years later, in the mid-eighteen-nineties, Kennelly was now collaborating with Edwin James Houston, a founder of the Thomson-Houston Company that eventually swallowed up Edison General Electric Company, to write several books extolling the benefits of alternating current.

Incidentally, Charles A. Coffin was the driving force that positioned Thomson-Houston Company to, effectively, take over Edison General Electric Company, with a decisive push by J. Pierpont Morgan. In 1892, while Latimer was quite busy in the leadership of Edison's legal department, Coffin became the first President of what was now called General Electric. He continued in that role or as Chairman until 1922.

Also at that exclusive Edison Pioneers luncheon at the Lawyers Club in Manhattan was George Francis Morrison. One of Thomas Edison's closest associates, who started at Edison Lamp Works in 1882 at the age of fifteen, Morrison had concentrated on the manufacture of electric lamps and their filaments. By the time of the luncheon, after several promotions, he was vice president of General Electric Company, heading GE's lamp business.

There are a few photos – all of them fading, grainy and in black and white – of the Edison Pioneers. Those assembled are generally conservatively-dressed men in the suits and top hats – when out of doors – in the style of the early twentieth century.

There's very little distinction between the men. But look more closely. Then you will see that one of the men is African American. It's Lewis Latimer of course, a member of this elite club of the nation's most accomplished men in the world's electrification. One can't help thinking how unusual it is that Latimer was so accepted in this highly-respected group of wealthy and famous men for the most part.

While Racism Raged

At a time that, for example, President Woodrow Wilson was happily viewing in the White House the racist film by D.W. Griffith, "Birth of a Nation," and overseeing the segregation of the federal government just a few months after his election. His Treasury Secretary, William McAdoo, was quoted defending the separating of the toilets in government agencies.

And then, in an infamous November 12, 1914 meeting with a delegation of African American leaders led by Harvard-educated William Monroe Trotter, an angry President Wilson said:

> "My question would be this: If you think that you gentlemen, as an organization, and all other Negro citizens of this country, that you are being humiliated, you will believe it. If you take it as a humiliation, which it is not intended as, and sow the seed of that impression all over the country, why the consequence will be very serious."

The President then threw Trotter out of his office, a man who had been a fervent political supporter in the election two years prior. The press went wild. The New York Times headline read, "President Resents Negro's Criticism." The New York Press headline went further, with the words, "Wilson Rebukes Negro Who 'Talks Up' to Him."

So Highly Respected by the Most Respected

Nonetheless, Latimer was clearly accepted as an equal by the elite Edison Pioneers, though you have to imagine that his white colleagues considered him unique. Their respect for Latimer is evident in the Edison Pioneers'

hand-typed and extensive obituary of December 11, 1928. Issued upon Latimer's death, and written by William Miron Meadowcroft, the group's historian, and the son of Edison's longtime personal secretary William Henry
Meadowcroft, it reads:

> "It was Mr. Latimer who executed the drawings and assisted in prepar-
> ing the applications for the telephone patents of Alexander Graham Bell."

And so, many of the leading scientists and engineers of the day had no
doubts as to Latimer's essential role in the telephone's invention, though Bell
himself didn't acknowledge this. They continued:

> "In 1880 he [Latimer] entered the employ of Hiram S. Maxim, Elec-
> trician of the United States Electric Lighting Company, then located in
> Bridgeport, Connecticut. It was while in this employ that Mr. Latimer
> successfully produced a method of making carbon filaments for the Max-
> im electric incandescent lamp, which he patented. His keen perception of
> the possibilities of the electric light and kindred industries resulted in his
> being the author of several other inventions."

This distinguished group had, additionally, no doubts as to Latimer's contributions to the development of electric lighting. Why otherwise would they
write this, or even admit Latimer as an equal, in a time when African Americans were so rarely treated as equals?

> "He was of the colored race, the only one in our organization, and was
> one of those to respond to the initial call that led to the formation of the
> Edison Pioneers, January 24th, 1918. Broadmindedness, versatility in the
> accomplishment of things intellectual and cultural, a linguist, a devoted
> husband and father, all were characteristic of him, and his genial presence
> will be missed from our gatherings … Mr. Latimer was a full member, and
> an esteemed one, of the Edison Pioneers."

The obituary is signed by the Edison Pioneers, at 40 West 40th Street in
New York City. This elite group was located in the prestigious and newly-built
American Radiator Building – later the American Standard Building and
now the Bryant Park Hotel – listed on the National Register of Historic Plac-
es and the subject of one of Georgia O'Keefe's skyscraper paintings, this one
completed a year before Latimer's passing. How many African Americans,

one wonders, had business in the American Radiator Building in the nineteen-twenties as a senior and broadly-respected stateman of American industry and technology as did Latimer?

Latimer's Movie, Almost

Latimer quite intentionally and successfully navigated in both the predominantly white and black society. He strived almost constantly to broaden his skills and to expand his impact in both worlds. One incredible episode exemplifies this.

In the fall of 1913, at the age of sixty-five, Latimer wrote a play and tried to have it turned into a movie. He had reason to believe this was a realistic possibility since Edison Studios made twelve hundred films in the twenty-five years of 1894 through the studio's closing in 1918. Indeed, the so-called Edison Trust – formerly the Motion Picture Patents Company – virtually monopolized the movie business until three years after Latimer's try at making a movie, in the fall of 1915, when Edison's monopoly was found guilty of antitrust violation.

It wasn't Latimer's first try at writing scripts. Thirteen years earlier he wrote a play entitled "Comedy," which was put on by the Brooklyn-based The Willing Workers Circle. The play earned him more than seventy-five dollars.

Latimer also had some of his poems and prose published, for which he received small fees. The editor of the popular British magazine The Leisure Hour said this to Latimer:

> "Let me tell you, poetry is your 'forte.' Every one of your poetic effusions ... Not only did they please me individually, but they have taken by storm every one that has read them."

Wanting to produce a movie, Latimer asked Edison's personal secretary, William Henry Meadowcroft, for his help. Meadowcroft, the personal secretary from 1910 to 1931, when Edison passed away, had previously been a lawyer and vice president of the Edison Electric Light Company.

He was a powerful voice, who authored the reverential biography of his boss, "The Boys' Life of Edison," and who could be expected to persuade Horace G. Plimpton, director of movie production at Edison Studios, to seriously consider Latimer's play for the silver screen. Plimpton had recently produced major motion pictures like "Frankenstein" in 1910, "The Battle of

**Edison Pioneers meet with Thomas Edison, including Lewis Latimer,
standing in the very front, at the far left.
Edison is the man standing with a cane in the front, second from the right.**

Trafalgar" in 1911, and "What Happened to Mary" and "The Land Beyond the Sunset" in 1912.

It would have been truly remarkable if Plimpton and Edison Studios had accepted Latimer's proposal and turned the play into a movie. After all, the first movie involving African Americans in its production would not come out for another six years, in 1919, when Oscar Micheaux's "The Homesteader" hit theaters. "A Fool and His Money," which was released in 1912, did have a black cast but it was headed by an all-white production team.

Latimer never did get his movie despite the vigorous attempt. Though the powerful Meadowcroft did write Latimer, notably addressing him as Dear Brother Latimer:

"It is quite unnecessary to say that I did the utmost that I could for you. Our people up there [at Edison Studios] have their own standards, and no one from here [in Edison's executive office] ever interferes with them or doubts their capacity to pass upon material which they themselves have to handle. If the matter should not go as you wish, do not be discourages {sic} but try again."

He had tried to be the first African American to write the screenplay for a motion picture. He had already authored one of the first technical books by an African American. And, he was arguably one of the nation's top experts in patents, plus a self-taught electrical engineer and draftsman. Pretty amazing for someone who had to leave school after the fifth grade because of his family's poverty. And, for someone who was alone in all settings, as far as we can tell, as a black professional in the rapidly-growing big business of electricity.

African America in the Late Twenties

In the late nineteen-twenties, when Latimer passed away, Americans followed the Sweet Trials in which the NAACP hired famed defense attorney Clarence Darrow to defend African American physician Ossian Sweet, who was charged with murder when a resentful and angry mob from his white Detroit neighborhood threatened violence and a Sweet friend fired from the house. American also followed the controversy surrounding the book and Broadway musical "Show Boat" about an interracial married couple.

Black-owned businesses were emerging and some thrived, particularly the North Carolina Mutual Life Insurance Company led by Charles Clinton

Spaulding. Twenty-six years younger than Lewis Latimer, Spaulding also helped lead the National Negro Insurance Association and National Negro Bankers Association. But, according to the U.S. Bureau of the Census, the majority of blacks were still employed in domestic and personal services, the iron, steel, textile, railroad and metal industries, and as general laborers.

In the sciences and engineering, there was Daniel Hale Williams who founded the first integrated hospital in the country, in Chicago, the first nursing school for African Americans, and performed the first successful heart surgery. As Latimer was the sole black member of the prestigious Edison Pioneers, Williams was the sole member of the American College of Surgeons. Williams was eight years younger than Latimer.

There was also Charles Henry Turner, nineteen years younger than Latimer, who was apparently the first African American to earn a doctorate from the University of Chicago. Turner published forty-nine papers on honeybees, ants, cockroaches and other invertebrates including three articles in the journal "Science."

And, there was Garrett Augustus Morgan, Sr., twenty-nine years younger than Latimer, who invented the three-position traffic signal, a safety hood for firefighters, and successful hair products for blacks. Elijah J. McCoy was similarly a well-known and respected expert on technologies. Four years older than Latimer, his fifty-seven patents included an automatic lubricator for locomotive and ship steam engines, and a folding ironing board. Since Booker T. Washington knew both McCoy and Latimer, they likely knew each other or at least of each other. Railroad engineers came to embrace the locomotive steam engine lubricator to such an extent that they coined the common expression, the "Real McCoy."

Chapter Six

The Meaning of Latimer Today

My Own Journey, and Racism

I have occasionally wondered what it would be like to talk with Lewis Latimer. Just suppose that I could have sat down with this great man near the end of his time, sometime in 1927 or in the months of 1928 before he passed away at the age of eighty.

Perhaps he would have allowed me to visit him at his home on Holly Avenue, in the Flushing section of Queens, New York. His eyesight failing by then, the room surrounded by musical instruments and paintings, evidence of his love of the arts, I believe his intrinsic kindness and intellectual curiosity would have shone through just as brightly as earlier in his remarkable life. And, together for an hour or two, we would reflect on his accomplishments and the challenges and stresses he overcame, always with his indefatigable optimism.

Latimer was an extraordinary man who was in the middle of so many historic developments of the period. This alone merits telling his incredible story as this book attempts. But the real motivation of this author is to unravel the mysteries of how vital Latimer actually was in inventing the modern world. And, then, to apply what we surmise to the dynamics of race and racism in the here and now, in the early twenty-first century, a hundred and forty-four years after Alexander Graham Bell, Thomas Watson and Lewis Latimer collaborated to complete the telephone patent application.

Self-Improvement

Latimer fervently believed in the value of self-improvement. It's not an exaggeration to posit that self-improvement defined him. He taught himself industrial drawing, from a base of no training whatsoever. And, then he taught himself electrical engineering, again only by observing the engineers around him, and as always, reading voraciously.

That's how he taught himself patent law. He willed himself to learn foreign languages, to be more effective in his work:

"We began to extend our business and I went with Mr. Maxim to Philadelphia to assist him in putting in a plant in the Philadelphia Ledger office. After fitting up this plant I was dispatched to Montreal Canada to fit up the railroad station and yards of Hochelage with incandescent and arc lamps.

As all of our assistants were French speaking natives I had to write out a list of such orders as I must use to make clear to my work men what I wanted them to do, and these orders I had to have the clerk teach me to express in French. This was my nightly lesson. My day was spent climbing telegraph poles and locating arc lamps on them with the assistance of my laborers who seemed much impressed with my effort to speak their native language."

His self-taught proficiency in French and German was so strong the Edison Companies often depended upon these skills of his. And who did Edison's men entrust to keep their all-important library? Why, Latimer of course. Later, he became a strong reader of Latin and Greek.

All the while, Latimer endeavored to infuse the civil rights movement of the turn of the century and early twentieth century with this philosophy of self-improvement, as did other leaders of the African American community, most famously his friend Booker T. Washington. African American leader W.E.B. Du Bois vehemently opposed this civil rights approach by Washington and others in his camp such as Latimer. Du Bois wrote in his 1934 book, "Black Reconstruction in America":

"This brings us to the situation when Booker T. Washington became the leader of the Negro race and advised them to depend upon industrial education and work rather than politics. The better class of Southern Negroes stopped voting for a generation. Then with the shift of population toward the North, there comes the present situation when out of 12,000,000 Negroes, 3,000,000 are in the North and 9,000,000 in the South. Those in the North and in the Border States vote. Those in the South are seriously restricted in their voting, and this restriction means that their political power is exercised by the white South, which gives the white South an extraordinary political influence as compared with the voters of the North and East."

The Talent We've Missed

I've come to wonder, how many Lewis Latimers have we missed in America because their paths to achievement were so obstructed – from the results of racism – that their paths became impassable? I now wonder, too, how much brighter might be our world if just some of them could have had the opportunity to bring forth their ideas as had Latimer when he sat at his drafting table and drew the inventions of his and other brilliant minds?

We'll never know. There was no Negro Leagues for talented African Americans to advance technology as there was for talented African Americans to play baseball, before either were allowed to fully realize their potential, in baseball before Jackie Robinson joined the Brooklyn Dodgers in 1947.

That Latimer was permitted to contribute to technology's march is a testament to his brilliance and his almost inexplicable will to learn and succeed. In this regard he resembles the three great women portrayed in the book and movie "Hidden Figures," though his trials were a hundred years earlier than those of Mary Jackson, Katherine Johnson and Dorothy Vaughn at NASA.

Controversies Black and White About Latimer's Legacy

There have been reasoned and unreasonable arguments about how much Lewis Latimer actually contributed to the invention of the telephone and electric lighting.

On the Internet, where the broadest range of views and prejudices can be found, one can see perspectives about the contributions of Latimer specifically and black inventors generally that border on racism and go beyond. The website blackinventionmyths.com is the most elaborate of this genre.

It's difficult to identify the authors of this rhetoric and their motivation. Contacting them leads to the commercial promotion of a service to potential inventors.

The website makes this argument:

"Perhaps you've heard the claims: Were it not for the genius and energy of African-American inventors, we might find ourselves in a world without traffic lights, peanut butter, blood banks, light bulb filaments, and a vast number of other things we now take for granted but could hardly imagine life without.

Such beliefs usually originate in books or articles about black history. Since many of the authors have little interest in the history of technology outside of advertising black contributions to it, their stories tend to be fraught with misunderstandings, wishful thinking, or fanciful embellishments with no historical basis. The lack of historical perspective leads to extravagant overestimations of originality and importance: sometimes a slightly modified version of a pre-existing piece of technology is mistaken for the first invention of its type; sometimes a patent or innovation with little or no lasting value is portrayed as a major advance, even if there's no real evidence it was ever used.

Unfortunately, some of the errors and exaggerations have acquired an illusion of credibility by repetition in mainstream outlets, especially during Black History Month (see examples for the traffic light and ironing board). When myths go unchallenged for too long, they begin to eclipse the truth. Thus I decided to put some records straight. Although this page does not cover every dubious invention claim floating around out there, it should at least serve as a warning never to take any such claim for granted."

More respected observers also sow doubt about the accuracy of histories of black achievement such as of Lewis Latimer's role in late nineteenth century inventions. In particular, the well-read historian Arthur Schlesinger, Jr. has occasionally railed against African American historians and educators that try to put a greater emphasis on the contributions to the progress of civilization by women and men of color. In his "The Disuniting of America: Reflections on a Multicultural Society," revised and re-published in 1998, he criticizes a story sometimes told of the accidental death of the great black scientist Charles Richard Drew, who improved the storage of blood, saving many lives of Allied forces during World War II.

The story's origin? An episode of the television show M*A*S*H. Yet, Schlesinger cites this story as evidence that so-called Afro-centrist ideologues make dubious claims to exaggerate the contributions of those of African origin. But in so doing, Schlesinger does a disservice to a great black scientist whose contributions do indeed merit greater emphasis in our histories and our education of young Americans, of all origins.

Perhaps, Schlesinger would want to perpetuate the inaccuracy in our histories and education of the young that Alexander Graham Bell alone invented the telephone and Thomas Edison alone invented the light bulb. In doing so, he diminishes the simultaneous inventions by Elisha Gray and Hiram Maxim. And, he disregards the essential role of the men who worked with Bell and Edison, including the extraordinary African American who helped both (and Maxim too), Lewis Latimer.

Latimer's Identity as an African American

Notwithstanding how well Latimer fit into American business and society, and notwithstanding the criticisms by blacks who advocated accelerated change in how the country confronted racism, Latimer was always aware of his African American background and perspectives. And, he was always aware in his later years of his added responsibility as a role model, as the most successful black in industry and technology to that point in history.

One of his poems, Ebon Venus, illustrates his proud racial identity:

Let others boast of maidens fair,
Of eyes of blue and golden hair;
My heart like needles ever true
Turns to the maiden of ebon hue.
I love her form of matchless grace,
The dark brown beauty of her face,
Her lips that speak of love's delight,
Her eyes that gleam as stars at night.
O'er marble Venus let them rage,
Who sets the fashions of the age;
Each to his taste, but as for me,
My Venus shall be ebony.

The poem was published in 1890 in New York Age, a black-owned newspaper. It's the same year Latimer's book "Incandescent Electric Lighting" was published by D. Van Nostrand Company, a mainstream house that issued scientific and engineering texts. Again, Latimer knew few bounds and crossed many boundaries.

After Latimer's death in 1928, the weekly black-owned Amsterdam News printed these words in its pages:

"His work in science was an achievement and his personal life was a work of art."

In that same week, the New York Times printed these words reporting his passing:

"Lewis H. Latimer, an electrical engineer widely known throughout the United States and a member of the Edison Pioneers, died on Tuesday night at his home ... He drew for Alexander Graham Bell the original plans of the telephone."

The Times apparently didn't consider it necessary to note in the article the race of this special man.

References

All Ideas are Second-Hand: Mark Twain's Magnificent Letter to Helen Keller About the Myth of Originality, by Maria Popova, www.brainpickings.org.

Arguing Until Doomsday, Stephen Douglas, Jefferson Davis, and the Struggle for American Democracy, by Michael E. Woods, 2020, The University of North Carolina Press.

Association of Edison Illuminating Companies, 1893 annual meeting minutes.

Barnum, An American Life, by Robert Wilson, 2019, Simon & Schuster Paperbacks.

Bell, Alexander Graham Bell and the Conquest of Solitude, by Robert V. Bruce, 1973, Cornell University Press.

Birthday Party to Edison, Men Associated with Him in the Early 80s Organize the Pioneers, The New York Times, February 3, 1918.

Black Inventors in the Age of Segregation, by Rayvon Fouche, 2003, The Johns Hopkins University Press.

Black Men in Navy Blue During the Civil War, Part 2, by Joseph P. Reidy, National Archives, Fall 2001, Vol. 33, No. 3.

Black Reconstruction in America, An Essay Towards a History of the Part Which Black Folk Played in the Attempt to Reconstruct Democracy in America, 1860-1880, by W.E.B. Du Bois, Edited by Henry Louis Gates, 2006, Oxford University Press.

Blueprint for Change: The Life and Times of Lewis H. Latimer, 1995, Queens Borough Public Library.

Charles G. Perkins, by Edward J. Covington, www.lamptech.co.uk.

Crusade for Justice, the Autobiography of Ida B. Wells, Edited by Alfreda M. Duster, 1970, 2020, The University of Chicago Press.

Death of Luther Stieringer, Electrical World and Engineer, 1903.

Edison, 71, Honored by Old Associates, "Edison Pioneers," at Luncheon, Express Their Pride in Inventor's Patriotic Occupation, The New York Times, February 12, 1918.

Edison, A Life of Invention, by Paul Israel, 1998, John Wiley & Sons, Inc.

Edison Electric Light Company Vs. F.P. Little Electrical Construction and Supply Company Et Al: On Letters Patent No. 281,576, Circuit Court of the United States for the Northern District of New York, 1896.

Edison's Electric Light, by Francis R. Upton, an article in Scribner's Monthly, February 1880, Scribner & Co.

Electric Incandescent Lighting, by Edwin J. Houston and A.E. Kennelly, 1896, The W.J. Johnston Company.

Electrical Exhibitors at the St. Louis Exposition, American Electrician, June 1904.

'Fearsome and Intimidating' Texts, The New York Times, November 18, 1987, excerpting a report entitled "American History Textbooks: An Assessment of Quality" by Gilbert T. Sewall.

Guide to the William J. Hammer Collection, Electricity and Modern Physics Division, Archives Center, National Museum of American History.

Hidden Figures, The American Dream and the Untold Story of the Black Women Mathematicians Who Helped Win the Space Race, by Margot Lee Shatterly, 2016, William Morrow.

How the 1876 Election Effectively Ended Reconstruction, by Sara Pruitt, January 21, 2020, www.history.com.

Illusions of Emancipation, The Pursuit of Freedom & Equality in the Twilight of Slavery, by Joseph P. Reidy, The University of North Carolina Press.

"I shall have him to dine as often as I please" – The time when Roosevelt invited African-American educator Booker T. Washington to a dinner at the White House, by Goran Blazeski, November 22, 2016, thevintagenews.com.

Incandescent Electric Lighting, A Practical Description of the Edison System, by L.H. Latimer, C.J. Field and John White Howell, 1890, D. Van Nostrand Company.

Inspirational Black History Draws Academic Fire, by Suzanne Daley, The New York Times, October 10, 1990.

Inventing a Better Life: Latimer's Technical Career, 1880-1928, by Bayla Singer, edison.rutgers.edu.

Lewis Howard Latimer, by Edward J. Covington, www.lamptech.co.uk.

Lewis Howard Latimer, Pioneers in Change, by Glennette Tilley Turner, 1991, Silver Burdett Press.

Lewis Latimer, Black Americans of Achievement, by Winifred Latimer Norman and Lily Patterson, 1994, Chelsea House Publishers.

Lewis H. Latimer House, by Gale Harris of the Landmarks Preservation Commission, 1995.

Memoirs of John Quincy Adams: Comprising Portions of His Diary From 1795 to 1848, Volume 11, by John Quincy Adams.

Menlo Park Reminiscences, Volume One, by Francis Jehl, 1936, The Edison Institute.

Menlo Park Reminiscences, Volume Two, by Francis Jehl, 1938, The Edison Institute.

Menlo Park Reminiscences, Volume Three, by Francis Jehl, 1941, The Edison Institute.

Not Made for Black History Month, Lewis Latimer and Technological Assimilation, by Rayvon Fouche, a chapter of Appropriating Technology: Vernacular Science and Social Power, edited by Roy Eglash, Jennifer L. Croissant, Giovanna Di Chiro, and Rayvon Fouche, 2004, University of Minnesota Press.

Obituary of Lewis Howard Latimer, December 11, 1928, W.E.B. Du Bois Papers, University of Massachusetts Amherst Libraries.

Petition Signed by Thomas A. Edison for Sunday Openings at the World's Columbian Exposition, National Archives.

Photography of the Invisible and Its Value in Surgery, by Tal Golan, September 24, 2015, Circulating Now, from the Historical Collections of the National Library of Medicine.

Reconstruction, America's Unfinished Revolution, 1863-1877, by Eric Foner, 1988, 2014, Harper Perennial.

Separate, The Story of Plessy v. Ferguson, and America's Journey from Slavery to Segregation, by Steve Luxenberg, 2019, W.W. Norton & Company.

The Amazing Hiram Maxim, An Intimate Biography, by Arthur Hawkey, 2001, Spellmount Limited.

The Black Cabinet, The Untold Story of African Americans and Politics During the Age of Roosevelt, by Jill Watts, 2020, Grove Press.

The Boys' Life of Edison, by William H. Meadowcroft, 1911, Harper & Brothers Publishers.

The Disuniting of America, Reflections on a Multicultural Society, by Arthur M. Schlesinger, Jr., Revised and Enlarged Edition, 1998, W.W. Norton & Company.

The Field of Blood, Violence in Congress and the Road to Civil War, by Joanne B. Freeman, 2018, Picador.

The case of George Latimer, in an anti-slavery newspaper, www.rarenewspapers.com.

The George Latimer Case: A Benchmark in the Struggle for Freedom, by Asa J. Davis, edison.rutgers.edu.

The Life and Times of Wendell Phillips, by George Lowell Austen, 1888, Lee and Shepard Publishers.

The Manufacture of Carbons for Electric Lighting and Other Purposes; a Practical Handbook, Giving a Complete Description of the art of Making Carbons, Electrodes, [etc.], the Various gas Generators and Furnaces Used in Carbonising; With a Plan for a Model, by Francis Jehl, 1899, Benn Brothers, Limited.

The Myth of the Sole Inventor, by Mark A. Lemley, Michigan Law Review, 2012, Volume 110, Issue 5.

The Slaughterhouse Cases: Interpreting the Reconstruction Amendments, by Jonathan Stahl, Constitution Daily, October 19, 2015, constitutioncenter.org.

The Thomas A. Edison Papers, Rutgers School of Arts and Sciences, Paul B. Israel, Director and General Editor.

The War Before the War, Fugitive Slaves and the Struggle for America's Soul from the Revolution to the Civil War, by Andrew Delbanco, 2018, Penguin Books.

There is a North, Fugitive Slaves, Political Crisis, and the Cultural Transformation in the Coming of the Civil War, by John L. Brooke, 2019, University of Massachusetts Press.

United States Census, multiple years.

United States Patent Office, the many patents cited in this book.

USS Massasoit, The Siege of Petersburg Online, www.beyondthecrater.com.

Weston vs. Latimer vs. Edison, Interference: Electric Lamps, In the United States Patent Office, 1885.

Where Discovery Sparks Imagination, A Pictorial History of Radio and Electricity, by John D. Jenkins, 2009, The American Museum of Radio and Electricity.

William Johnson Jenks Obituary, IEEE Institute Affairs, 1918.

Wilmington's Lie, The Murderous Coup of 1898 and the Rise of White Supremacy, by David Zucchino, 2020, Atlantic Monthly Press.

Index